Forever in
Joy

Forever in Joy

THE LIFE OF ROBERT BROWNING

by

Rosemary Sprague

CHILTON BOOK COMPANY

PHILADELPHIA   NEW YORK   LONDON

To Samuel Claggett Chew
and Finley Melville Kendall Foster
Teachers and Friends

ACKNOWLEDGMENTS

I wish to thank Houghton Mifflin Company for permission to quote from Nathaniel Hawthorne's *Passages from French and Italian Notebooks* and also from *The Letters of Charles Eliot Norton,* edited by Sara Norton and M. Q. DeWolfe Howe; E. P. Dutton Company, Inc., for permission to quote from *Carlyle in Old Age (1865–1881)* by D. A. Wilson and D. W. Macarthur; and Gardner B. Taplin for permission to quote from *The Life of Elizabeth Barrett Browning* (Yale University Press).

I would also like to thank Sir John Murray for permission to quote from *The Letters of Robert Browning and Elizabeth Barrett Browning; Letters of Robert Browning Collected by T. J. Wise,* edited by Thurman L. Hood; *Twenty-Two Unpublished Letters of Elizabeth Barrett Browning and Robert Browning, Addressed to Henrietta and Arabella Moulton Barrett; New Letters of Robert Browning,* edited by William Clyde DeVane and Kenneth Leslie Knickerbocker; and *Dearest Isa: Robert Browning's Letters to Isabella Blagden,* edited by Edward C. McAleer.

I would additionally like to thank Chapman & Hall, Ltd., for permission to quote from *The Diaries of William Charles Macready, 1833–51;* and Methuen & Company, Ltd., for permission to quote from *The Life of Robert Browning* by W. Hall Griffin and Harry Christopher Minchin.

And, I would like to thank Dr. Joseph Ashbrook, editor of *Sky and Telescope Magazine,* for assistance in verifying astronomical fact and for dissipating astronomical myth.

FOREWORD

Robert Browning did not want his biography to be written. During his lifetime he categorically refused permission to all who asked the privilege, and he was equally adamant about refusing to write his own memoirs. He was, of course, aware that biographies would be inevitable after his death, but he destroyed much of his early work and a major portion of his personal papers, to prevent their falling into unsympathetic hands. The biographer of Browning is, therefore, faced with a unique situation—a major literary figure who is tremendously difficult to document. It is this situation which has given rise to the numerous Browning myths, and to *post-hoc* Freudian interpretations of his poetry, in an effort to understand the poet as a man.

In order to avoid either of these errors, I have tried as far as possible to depend upon Browning's own correspondence that is left to us. I have also consulted the biography written shortly after his death by his close friend, Mrs. Sutherland Orr, and the biography compiled by W. H. Griffin in 1910 and revised by Harry C. Minchin in 1938, as being the two secondary sources nearest to the poet in time, and thus likely to be the most factually accurate. Occasionally, however, I have had to indulge in "educated surmises." For background material about Elizabeth Barrett Browning, I am greatly indebted to Professor Gardiner Taplin's excellent biography of her.

But it is Browning's poetry, in itself, which provides the best key to his character and personality—provided it is read against the background of Victorian England. A poet must be of his own time before he can be of all time, and to read Browning in isolation, so to speak, would be fatal. So I have not hesitated to include historical material where relevant, pertinent, and enlightening. Browning was completely involved in his own world, religiously, politically, creatively; he knew it, understood it, and loved it. Perhaps that is why he speaks so vibrantly and pointedly to our world, which seems far removed from Victorian England, but is, actually, in essentials, very little different from the world he knew.

ROSEMARY SPRAGUE

"How good is man's life, the mere living! How fit to
    employ
All the heart and soul and the senses forever in joy!"

—"Saul"

1

It is true that a fiery comet blazed over England on the night of May 7, 1812. But in the house in Southampton Street, Camberwell, one of the new suburbs of London, no one was especially interested in this phenomenon. Any passer-by could have known, by the light dimly visible behind the drawn curtains of the upstairs bedroom and the doctor's carriage waiting at the curb, that the Browning family had far more important concerns that evening, which were confirmed a few days later, when R. Browning, Esquire, wrote in the flyleaf of the family Bible, "Robert Browning, born May 7th, 1812."

The entry was the traditional one for such occasions. Its position directly below the entry of Mr. Browning's marriage to Sarah Anna Wiedemann in February of the preceding year indicated that Robert was the first-born son and eldest child. It was neither the custom nor in the province of such entries to give more than essential fact. Neither statement indicates in the slightest the turbulent background of the Browning marriage, nor the equally turbulent world into which Robert was born; but this turbulence on both counts was, nevertheless, both an integral part of the poet's character and a profound influence on his life.

All the biographies of Robert Browning begin by emphasizing the serenity and security of his early childhood environment, nor are they mistaken in so doing. Camberwell was a typical country village in 1812, in an England still green and pleasant, uninvaded by railroads, uncrowded by factories. When the family moved, after the arrival of Robert's sister Sariana in 1814, and again in 1824, it was not a matter of moving into the country to escape the city, but simply of moving, in each instance, to a larger residence on Southampton Street. All the houses in Camberwell had green grass plots and trees in front, and large gardens in the rear. Nearby was Dowlas Common, and beyond that the open fields where cricket was a regular Sunday afternoon diversion, and the old "Rosemary Branch" pub did a rushing business. Not far away was Dulwich Wood:

> Over head the tree-tops meet,
> Flowers and grass spring 'neath one's feet.

Robert Browning was to write twenty-nine years later in *Pippa Passes*. The action of that poem is set in Italy, but its landscape is pure turn-of-the century Camberwell.

So described, such an atmosphere seems far from turbulent and explosive, but this serenity is deceptive. In 1812, below her surface calm, England was both anxious and insecure. On May 9, two days after Robert's birth, Napoleon Bonaparte left Paris to join his *Grande Armée,* 600,000 conscripts strong, for his long dreamed-of invasion of Russia. England had already been drained of men for Wellington's army which had been rushed to the Peninsula to help the Spaniards in ousting Napoleon's brother Joseph, a puppet king wholly subservient to his brother's interests, whose incapacity as a ruler was equaled only by his capacity for wine. Now England watched aghast as "Boney" set out for Moscow, for no one in his right mind believed that the Tsar's colorful but unmilitarily minded troops would be any match for the victor of Austerlitz and Jena. And when Napoleon, as he had already prophesied and boasted, would have all Europe from Siberia to the

Atlantic under his thumb, how could England stand against him? Even nature seemed to augur in his favor: that fiery comet with a tail one hundred million miles long had been constantly visible in Europe for over a year before it had blazed across England on the night of May 7. Had not Napoleon constantly maintained that his destiny was written in the stars? Robert Browning later said humorously that the great comet had been an augury of his own destiny, but on May 9, 1812, all England, including the poet's parents, saw in it only an omen of everyone's ultimate destruction.

As though Napoleon were not enough, England was also in the grip of violent labor unrest. Much of the nation's economy depended on the cotton weaving industry centered in the great Lancashire and Yorkshire mills. The mills, in turn, depended upon raw cotton imported from America; and America, already justly provoked at British impressment on the high seas of American citizens for service in the royal navy, and wishing to avoid possible difficulties with France, had cut off all commerce with England. The embargo had thrown thousands of cotton spinners and weavers out of work. Angry men and women, unimpressed by political considerations and seeking for something on which to blame their plight, marched on the factories, smashing the power looms and spinning jennies, which, ironically, were as idle as they, though they maintained that the machines had destroyed their livelihoods. Stringent measures had to be taken to quell what had become full-scale rioting. A special constabulary was sworn in; the yeomanry of the counties involved were called to active duty and an armed camp was set up in Sherwood Forest. Nor did London escape the effects of this civil disorder. On May 11, the prime minister, Spencer Perceval was assassinated as he addressed the House of Commons!

For several weeks thereafter the city lived under near martial law, and order had scarcely been restored when, in June, America declared war. By September, Napoleon, victorious at Borodino, had occupied Moscow. True, "General Winter" forced his retreat, but this afforded the world little respite. "Boney's" phenomenal luck held long enough for him to reconstitute his army, and, in the early spring of 1813, he was battling a coalition of Russia, England, and Prussia on the Rhine. The first months of Robert Browning's life were filled with the pounding of gunnery practice, tolling alarm bells, and the tramping of men marching north to defend England against the cotton rioters or south to Portsmouth to ship out for service in Spain, Germany, or America.

All this upheaval, which was to continue until the Battle of Waterloo in June, 1815, could not but have had its effect upon every man, woman, and child, even the most ordinary and unheedful. But Robert Browning was neither ordinary nor unheeding, nor were his parents, though his father was then a clerk in the Bank of England, a prosaic enough occupation. As a very young man, R. Browning, Esquire, had been sent out to St. Kitt's in the West Indies, to take charge of a sugar plantation which he had inherited from his mother. He had become incensed by the slave system of labor there and had returned to England. His father, the poet's grandfather, having meanwhile made a second marriage, greeted his eldest son with rage for repudiating a fortune because of scruples which he, apparently, did not share, and put him to work at the bank where he himself was an officer. R. Browning, Esquire, would have preferred to be an artist, a profession for which he had considerable aptitude if not a major talent, but his gentle sensitivity was no match for his father's irascibility. His work at the bank did not destroy his love of painting, however, nor his love of books. A devoted bibliophile, he acquired a personal library of over six thousand rare volumes, and in this library he spent many of his leisure hours. The sight of his father engrossed in a book is one of Robert Browning's earliest memories:

> My Father was a scholar and knew Greek.
> When I was five years old, I asked him once
> "What do you read about?" "The seige of Troy."
> "What is a seige, and what is Troy?"
>
> *Asolando:* "Development"

The poet goes on to tell how his father dramatized the event for him, and how "The Seige of Troy" became one of his favorite childhood games. R. Browning, Esquire, though not a University man, was a superb classical scholar, and his knowledge of old French, Spanish, and Italian literature was remarkable and quite unusual, even for a university man of his time. Robert fully recognized and respected these abilities and frequently consulted him for background information to use in his poetry. In 1866, in his father's eighty-fifth year, he wrote to a friend,

> His mind is absolutely as I always remember it, and
> the other day when I wanted some information
> about a point of medieval history, he wrote a
> regular book of notes and extracts thereabout.[1]

No portrait survives of Sarah Wiedemann Browning, the poet's mother. But, since sons are supposed to resemble and "take after" their mothers, and Robert Browning was considered one of the handsomest men of his time, she was undoubtedly very attractive, as well as highly intelligent. Her father, the son of a German shipowner, had settled in Dundee, Scotland, and had married a Scotswoman; but Sarah and her sister Christiana were living with an uncle at Camberwell when she met R. Browning, Esquire, lately returned from the West Indies. Many years later, Robert Browning wrote of his parents' courtship to Elizabeth Barrett—how his grandfather, hearing of his son's interest in young Miss Wiedemann, had "benevolently waited upon her uncle to assure him that his niece would be thrown away on a man so evidently born to be hanged!—these were his very words." [2] The senior Browning had had his way about the Bank of England; he did not, however, have his way about the marriage. Ultimately he was reconciled to it, though he took his time about permitting himself any pride and pleasure in his daughter-in-law and grandchildren.

Sarah Browning was what might be described as a typical Victorian wife and mother, a quarter of a century before Victoria came to the throne. Her province was to manage her home expertly and to raise her children properly, which she did with prudence and considerable grace. Thomas Carlyle described her as the true type of Scottish gentlewoman, and a cousin said of her that a woman like her had no need to go to heaven, for she made heaven wherever she found herself. This kind of praise perhaps strikes discordantly on twentieth century ears, but in 1812 a woman was not expected to be "fourth-dimensional," or to participate publicly in crusades for civic betterment. The "betterment" in which she engaged required unselfish personal sacrifice, which she made quietly and gladly. Sarah Browning was a supremely happy woman, worshiped by her husband and adored by her children, and this was all any woman of her time wanted or asked.

If her husband was the head of the house, she was its heart and the guardian of its spiritual and aesthetic values. She was devoutly evangelical and truly religious. She loved her garden and made it one of the showplaces of Camberwell. She was also an extraordinarily good pianist, and her son later remembered how, as a small boy, her music could bring tears to his eyes. This emotional reaction always distressed Mrs. Browning, who would stop playing, only to have him rush to her and bury his face in her skirts, sobbing insistently, "Play! Play!" It was she who did most of the reading aloud when her children were small; Robert loved the poems of Byron and *Paradise Lost* above all else. He also enjoyed *Robinson Crusoe*. But sometimes her choice was not approved. There was a book called Croxall's *Fables*, a highly edifying, moral volume in the style of Aesop. Robert loved animals—he had his own menagerie, including a hedgehog and two large snakes—and he liked to hear about them. But the story about the lion being kicked to death by a donkey affected him so deeply that he conceived a violent antagonism for Croxall, and he disposed of the book by hiding it between the upholstery and the woodwork of a large chair.

That the Brownings had a very close family relationship is obvious, but it was not at all restrictive. Good manners and filial respect were insisted upon; as long as his parents lived, Robert, whenever he was with them, never failed to bid them good-night in the manner considered proper for sons of the day and age. His parents, for their part, recognized early that they had a most unusual son. He admitted that he was born "supremely passionate." He had a violent temper and a very strong will. These his parents did their best to curb and direct, but they put no rein on his imagination which evidenced itself almost as soon as he could talk. When, at the age of three, he put a fine length of Brussels lace into the fire and called to his mother to see the "pitty baze," she reprimanded him sternly; but when he entertained her with a fantastic account of what he had seen on a walk, she did not scold him for untruthfulness. She merely remarked humorously, "Why, sir, you are quite a geographer!" His father had a talent for versifying extemporaneously, a favorite form of Victorian parlor entertainment, and Robert quickly learned to imitate him, striding round and round the table and making up verses of his own. No one ever knew when he began to read, nor when he began to write poetry. His earliest attempts were imitation Byron or wild Ossianic rant, but there was one which he wrote about Napoleon Bonaparte when he was about eight or nine—probably nine, since Bonaparte died in May, 1821, and Robert Browning was always sensitive to the immediate current event. The poem was later destroyed, but his father said years later that it had been unbelievably good for a child. That he wrote such a poem so early indicates his sensitive awareness of the world around him; it also indicates that, though he had doubtless been raised to abhor Napoleon the tyrant dictator, he felt a secret affection for Napoleon the fallen hero and soldier, which explains the singularly sympathetic treatment which he gave of "Boney" in one of his most stirring dramas in miniature, "Incident of the French Camp."

He was sent to school before he was five. A lady "of reduced circumstances" had established a small school in her Camberwell home to teach the rudiments of reading, writing, and ciphering. Here Robert progressed so quickly that he soon outstripped all his classmates, even the eldest. Mothers complained that the teacher was neglecting their children in favor of Master Browning, so she, though heartbroken at losing such a brilliant pupil, had to ask the Brownings to remove their son from her school. For the next two years he was tutored at home; then, at the age of eight, he was sent to a preparatory school, directed by the Reverend Thomas Ready at Peckham.

Peckham was only a mile from Camberwell, so Robert was entered as a weekly boarding pupil, returning home for Saturday and Sunday. His experience at school was not altogether happy. Admittedly he was intellectually far in advance of other boys his age and of many of the older boys, as well; in fact, it is quite possible that, in some respects, he was a fair match for Mr. Ready. But it is equally true that his education up to now had not included classroom discipline and submitting to it irked him considerably.

> . . . Long restraint chained down
> My soul . . .

he complained in his first long poem, *Pauline,* though just how much of the complaint is truth, and how much exaggeration or self-sympathy, is open to conjecture. Various of his classmates later recalled his look of almost angelic propriety in his brown Holland linen smock, the small boy's uniform in 1820, but they also attested to the fact that he was far from angelic in behaviour. He had a wicked wit, and a talent for writing barbed epigrams:

> A *heavy* sermon—sure, the error's great,
> For not a word Tom utters has its weight.

was his comment on one of the headmaster's sermons. Mr. Ready had two sisters who acted as matrons, or housemothers, and they used to sing hymns while brushing the boys' hair, a habit which Robert burlesqued with gusto. There was also a secret departure from school by night to see London illuminated by the newly installed gas lamps. His academic brilliance saved him from more stringent punishment than an occasional box on the ear, and he always passed his grades, but he seems to have made a point of not taking any prizes.

In fact he was, as he later ruefully admitted, a quite arrogant, supercilious boy, and, not surprisingly, he made few friends at school. After his father's library, he found Mr. Ready's classroom dull and uninspiring. As for companionship with boys his own age, he had his cousins— James, John, and George Silverthorne, sons of his mother's sister—wild, gifted musicians who were as daring and eager for fun as he was himself. It is possible, too, that the chaotic world conditions, as well as the discipline enforced at school, also contributed to his restlessness. Though the Hundred Days were past, and Napoleon was safely imprisoned on St. Helena, there were student riots in Germany, revolutions in Italy and Spain, war between Russia and Persia, and labor riots in Glasgow. Byron had gone to Greece to help the revolution against Turkey and had died there in 1824. George IV now ruled England, and the world was being treated to the scandalous spectacle of a monarch's attempting to divorce his queen. Much as he loved Homer and Vergil and Horace, it was probably difficult for Robert to concentrate on Greek and Latin when there was so much excitement all around him.

Also, what other boy at school could boast of being a real poet at the age of twelve? He had compiled a volume of verses which he called *Incondita*, for which his parents tried to find a publisher. They were unsuccessful and Robert later destroyed the manuscript, but is was read and admired and praised by family friends. It brought him into contact with two intellectual ladies—his first literary friendships. The ladies were Sarah Flower Adams, a "poetess," still remembered for her hymn, "Nearer My

God to Thee," and her unmarried sister Eliza, a very attractive girl nine years older than Robert. Eliza was his first "attachment"; he wrote her long sentimental letters and poems, all of which he later destroyed. His idealization of her was that frequently felt by an adolescent boy for an "older woman"—certainly it could not be called a romance. In that era, young ladies were considered as angelic inspirations for young men, and Robert was as precocious in sentiment as he was in intellect. Also, a poet was *supposed* to have an inspiration. Eliza, for her part, encouraged his literary aspirations. If any one person inspired *Pauline,* it was most certainly she. As he grew older, his feeling matured into a warm, affectionate regard, which she reciprocated in kind, and, though he was ardently courting Elizabeth Barrett at the time, Eliza's death from consumption in 1846 grieved him deeply.

At the age of fourteen, having long since learned all Mr. Ready could teach him, Robert joyfully left school. The next two years he spent at home, studying with his father, reading all the books in the library he had not already read, visiting the newly opened Dulwich Art Gallery. He also studied Italian and French. London was full of refugees from the Napoleonic Wars who had turned to language teaching as a living, and while Mr. Browning was not a wealthy man, he was sufficiently well off to give his children all the advantages enjoyed by the Victorian upper-middle class. Sariana Browning had not been sent to school, for girls were customarily educated at home, but she studied languages with her brother, and was given painting and singing lessons as well. Robert had a marked talent for music, and was sent to study counterpoint with John Relfe, musician-in-ordinary to the king. Relfe had been a student of the Abbé Vogler, the celebrated organist, and it was through Relfe that Robert first learned of the remarkable *improvisateur* who would later become the subject of one of his finest poems. He studied piano under Abel, a student of the great pianist, Ignace Moschels. He tried his own hand at composing, setting some of Thomas Hood's lyrics and Donne's "Go, and catch a falling star" to music. He was given drawing lessons, too, and he learned to ride, box, dance, and fence. Removed from the limitations of the preparatory school classroom, he lost much of his superciliousness and arrogance, and he began to evidence that gift for friendship which was one of his most endearing characteristics as a man.

For such a young man, a university education was practically a necessity. The question was, how could he acquire it? The Brownings were not members of the Church of England, and no Dissenter might study at Cambridge or Oxford. And Robert was too forthright and honest to sign the Thirty-Nine Articles, pretending to subscribe to religious tenets which he could not conscientiously believe, merely to get a degree. So it was with great interest that his parents learned of the proposal for a new university in London, where membership in the established church would not be a requirement for admission. When the university became a reality in 1827, Mr. Browning promptly contributed one hundred pounds to the venture. In the summer of 1828, students were invited to make application for the autumn term, and the register under the date of June 16 was inscribed, "Robert Browning, age 16: Hanover Cottage, Southampton Street, nominated by Robert Browning, sr." Robert registered for courses in Greek, German, and Latin. Lodgings were found for him in Bedford Square, and his family looked forward in delighted anticipation to the day when their son would emerge as Robert Browning, Bachelor of Arts.

2

The new University of London was, to quote the *Times,* "a chaste and truly classic specimen of Greek architecture," though when Robert Browning arrived on opening day in October the cupola was non-existent, the portico was unfinished, and the faculty was not completely assembled. In a day when university education was synonymous with Oxford, Cambridge, and a tradition going back to the Middle Ages, this new building in Bloomsbury, shrieking of modernity and middle-class finance, was a blatant affront. Politically it leaned toward Whig liberalism; religiously, it was strictly non-sectarian to the point where the more orthodox considered it non-religious. For those who felt that young men who desired an education should have the opportunity to acquire one at tuition fees they could afford, the new institution symbolized a means of escape from the situations where rank, fortune, and religious orthodoxy had placed them. It was a way "to become a gentleman," a possible entrance to professions which had hitherto been closed, perhaps even, when the restrictive Liabilities Acts were repealed, a means by which a non-member of the Establishment might stand for election to the House of Commons. But to those who felt that a young man who, for whatever reason, could not go to Oxford or Cambridge should be content in the position where Providence had put him, the University of London was definitely suspect, and was quickly damned as the "Godless Institute of Gower Street."

Since religious observance was part of life in Robert

Browning's home, it did not immediately dawn on him that the new university was considered godless. Nor did it especially concern him. He had recently discovered Shelley, and had enthusiastically embraced him as a kindred spirit. Shelley had been a Liberal; then so was he. Shelley had believed in individual freedom; Browning proclaimed himself "vowed to liberty." Shelley had been an atheist; Browning greatly distressed his mother by announcing with lofty sixteen-year-old aplomb that he, too, was inclined to doubt the existence of God. "Sun-treader, life and light be thine forever!" he exulted four years later in *Pauline*, in which he recorded the effect that Shelley had had upon him in 1828. In later years he warned against his poems' being taken autobiographically; he admitted, however, that *Pauline* was a very personal work, and there is no doubt that he did go through a period of deep agnosticism, if not total atheism, leading to much soul-searching and longing for conviction that his fundamental beliefs were right.

> A mind like this must dissipate itself,
> But I have always had one lode-star; now,
> As I look back, I see that I have halted
> Or hastened as I looked towards that star—
> A need, a trust, a yearning after God . . .
> I felt as one beloved, and so shut in
> From fear; and thence I date my trust in signs
> And omens, for I saw God everywhere;
> And I can only lay it to the fruit
> Of a sad after-time that I could doubt
> Even his being—e'en the while I felt
> His presence, never acted from myself,
> Still trusted in a hand to lead me through
> All danger; and this feeling ever fought
> Against my weakest reason and resolve.

14

A religious crisis is frequently a phenomenon of adolescence, and Robert Browning's great sensitivity made his the more acute. As Shelley had done before him, he turned to a great "religion of humanity":

> Men were to be as gods and earth as heaven,
> And I—ah, what a life was mine to prove!
> My whole soul rose to meet it.

But inevitably disillusion came:

> First went my hopes of perfecting mankind,
> Next—faith in them, and then in freedom's self
> And virtue's self, then my own motives, ends
> And aims and loves, and human love went last.

He realized that his doubt, though honest, had led him to trust too much to his own rational powers, which, in turn, had brought him to that impasse where self-absorption and introspection made faith impossible.

> I'll look within no more.
> I have too trusted my vain self, vague intuition . . .

At the end of *Pauline,* he proclaimed his unshaken faith:

> Sun-treader, I believe in God and truth
> And love. . . .

the first declaration of his personal trinity—God, truth, and love—which was to become the basis of his personal creed.

At the time he entered the University of London, he was deep in the dark throes of unbelief, and this state of mind, coupled with the (to him) always irksome academic discipline, explains as well as any more tangible elements, his dissatisfaction with his new surroundings. Also, he was confronted by the same problem as at Mr. Ready's school; his questing mind and his eagerly demanded and absorbed reading had advanced him far beyond the other students. The courses of study, geared of necessity to their lesser capabilities, he found dull and uninspiring. And Bloomsbury Square, which Ruskin was to describe later as one of the ugliest parts of London, was just that, and bleak besides, compared to Camberwell. After one term he was convinced that this world was not for him, and he withdrew in the spring of 1829.

He was almost seventeen, but, by the standards of the day, he was already a man. Had his family insisted, they could have demanded that he earn his own living, but his father, remembering his own experience with the sugar plantation, was sympathetic and understanding. An offer was made to find a place at the bank for the erstwhile university student, but Mr. Browning rejected it as unworthy of his son's potentiality. He himself had been denied the artist's career he had wanted. Robert, whose ability was so much greater than his own, must have his chance to try his own wings. So, when opportunity arose for another connection, and Robert announced that it was his plan ". . . to look on real life, / That life all new to me," [1] no attempt was made to dissuade him.

A family friend, a retired sea captain named Pritchard, had a cousin, Dr. Blundell, who lectured at Guy's Hospital, and it was Captain Pritchard who presented Robert Browning to him. Browning enthusiastically attended Dr. Blundell's lectures for several months. He had no intention of becoming a doctor, but, after a world of books and paintings, the hospital seemed to offer the quickest, most direct contact with the "real life" he craved to experience. Perhaps he was also subconsciously imitating John Keats, the poet whom he admired most next to Shelley: Keats had trained for medicine before taking to poetry. Certainly Dr. Blundell was responsible for initiating his interest in science, a field hitherto unexplored, for neither school nor university curricula had included courses in science. Guy's Hospital did not occupy all of Browning's waking hours. He continued to study music and took up clay modeling. He made a foray into amateur theatricals in which he scored considerable success, for he possessed a good voice and was an excellent mimic. With his cousins, the Silverthornes, he made the rounds of art galleries, concert halls, and theaters. He especially enjoyed Shakespeare, and went several times to Drury Lane, where the great tragedian William Charles Macready was delighting London with his interpretation of Hamlet. This very pleasant life continued for three years, with Browning seemingly no nearer a decision as to what he really wished to do than when he had left the University of London. But he had matured greatly, though he did not realize how much.

When the moment of truth came, it came suddenly. Edmund Kean, one of the most brilliant actors ever to appear on the English stage, was performing in *Richard III* at a small theatre in Richmond. On the night of October 22, 1832, Robert Browning was in the audience. Kean, though still a comparatively young man, had broken his health through drink and dissipation, and his acting was no longer as powerful as it had been in his greatest days. Yet flashes of that power still came through occasionally, enough to overwhelm an uncritical audience in a provincial theatre, and Browning was so affected that he walked all the way home to Camberwell in a daze. The contrast between those glimpses of the actor who had been and the actor who now was, impressed him profoundly, and led him to ponder soberly his own life thus far. Admittedly, despite his seriousness about himself, he had done no serious work. Less kindly observers could justly dismiss him as a dilettante, living on his father's income, doing nothing to justify his existence. Further, he saw that his artificial, perverse religious doubts and constant self-analyzing were dissipating his own talent as surely as drink had ruined Kean's. If he really wanted to be a poet, it was time that he got to work. So, with the energy that characterized everything he did, he began at once to compose his first major poem. *Pauline, A Fragment of a Confession,* was completed in January, 1833.

This poem was intended to be the first of a series. Browning never dreamed in small terms, and his decision to make his first effort a series of long poems explaining the many facets of his "complex soul" was quite in character with his personality at that time. He quickly discovered, however, that no commercial publisher was interested in either his mysterious soul or his poetry. Perhaps the adverse critical and public reception of Tennyson's first volume, published the previous year, had made editors more chary toward another new poet. Also, a different kind of reader had developed by 1833, typically solid, respectably middle-class, to whom life was a serious business, and who looked with suspicion upon the excessive and emotional individualism of Byron, Shelley, Keats, and the other Romantics. Poetry, to please these new readers, must be beautiful, but it must also instruct. It must have a lesson, a message; it must inspire the reader to virtuous living. *Pauline* did none of these things, nor did Robert Browning, still in the throes of the Romantic ideal as set forth by Wordsworth—that poetry should be the spontaneous outflow of powerful feelings—intend that it should. He was disappointed and a little resentful at the lack of interest that greeted his work, but his parents encouraged him to continue trying to find a publisher, so he persevered. Finally Saunders and Otely agreed to undertake *Pauline*, provided he would pay the costs of printing. His aunt, Mrs. Silverthorne, advanced the money, and the book was published anonymously in March, 1833. Review copies were distributed, but *Pauline* was favorably noted by only a few critics and ignored by most. It achieved the dubious distinction of not selling a single copy.

Robert was devastated by the cold reception of his first effort, but fortunately he was not long in learning where part of its fault lay. John Stuart Mill, who would in twenty-five years' time achieve fame as a philosopher and as the author of *An Essay on Liberty*, was, in 1833, literary critic for the *Monthly Repository*. He had been given a copy of *Pauline* by the Reverend William Johnson Fox, guardian of Miss Eliza Flower (Browning's boyhood "literary inspiration"). Mill read *Pauline* four times, refused to review it in his magazine, and returned the copy to Fox with a long comment. He noted that the poem had much beauty in it, and that its psychological history was "powerful and truthful . . . the self-seeking and self-worshipping state are well described." [2] But he also pointed out most ruthlessly that the poem lacked conviction. That Browning had been too embroiled in his own emotions to write objectively, and, thus, much of the self-disgust emerged, to Mill at least, as thinly disguised self-pity. Fox handed this astringent comment to Browning, who read it, pondered it, and found it justified. He asked the publisher to return all the unbound sheets to him and he destroyed them. He disavowed *Pauline*, and thought no more of using poetry as a vehicle by which to explain his soul to the world. Not until 1847, when Dante Gabriel Rossetti, rummaging in the British Museum, found a lone copy and taxed Browning with its authorship, did Browning acknowledge it, but he did not permit it to be included in his collected works until 1868, and then only after revision.

And from 1833 on, his poetry was, for the most part, written as though spoken by voices other than his own. For him to speak in his own voice, he had decided, was dangerous; it tempted him, as Mill had caustically pointed out, to the luxury of self-pity. It did not reveal; it exposed. Other poets might pour out their own souls on paper, but he would speak for other men and women. The dramatic monologue, the form which he brought to perfection, was born in his repudiation of *Pauline*. He had had some experience in the theatre in donning the actor's mask. So in his poetry should a mask conceal him from the world on the printed page.

Mill's comment dampened his ardor for the time being, and the projected series of long poems was laid aside. So when, early in 1834, he was invited by George de Benkhausen, the Russian consul-general, to accompany him as his secretary on a special mission to St. Petersburg, he accepted with alacrity. No one has ever discovered how the two men became acquainted, but it is reasonable to suppose that De Benkhausen must have been interested in art and literature, for Browning, apart from being "vowed to liberty," had no particular political convictions or affiliations. Captain Pritchard may have had something to do with their meeting. He and Browning were members of an informal club called the "Colloquials," another member of which was Alfred Domett, a young poet whose first volume had also been published in 1833, with better success than Browning's *Pauline*. In a poem called "Waring," described as a "fancy portrait of a very dear friend"—i.e., Domett—Browning imagines him as visiting Russia. Care must be taken not to read too much autobiography into any Browning poem, but it seems odd that he would place his absent friend in Russia, and, further, disguise him under the name of Waring, a king's messenger whom he had met at St. Petersburg, if there had not been some connection in his own mind between Domett and Russia. Also, Domett's father, who had been one of Nelson's captains, was a prominent lawyer, and his son's later distinguished career in New England politics argues some family acquaintance with political and diplomatic circles in England. Pritchard, too, had connections in the same circles, so it is highly possible that Browning's acquaintance with De Benkhausen was initiated by him.

The precise nature of De Benkhausen's mission is also unknown. It may have been in regard to Russia's annexation of Poland, or he may have been carrying one of England's several diplomatic protests against the current Russian treaty with the sultan of Turkey, an agreement considered most inimical to English interests in the Near East. Browning, however, was probably not too deeply concerned with the political aspects of the journey. The journey itself was excitement enough, for, after the packet boat docked at Rotterdam, he had to travel by coach and horseback fifteen hundred miles across Prussia and into a cold, snowbound land where few travelers from western Europe ever ventured.

> Through forestry right and left, black verst and verst of pine,
> From village to village runs the road's long wide bare line,

he remembered, when he came to write "I, the came to write "Ivàn Ivànovitch" in 1879. Over snow "glib as ice and hard as steel," he galloped, stopping at the inns in the infrequent villages for a change of horses and a few hours' rest, then on to Peter the Great's fabulous city, where the marble palaces built in eighteenth-century neo-classic style contrasted sharply with the painted and gilded onion-domed churches that he and the greater part of the world had seen only in pictures. He saw a fair on the River Neva, where the ice was so thick that hawkers could set their booths up on it without danger, and even horse-drawn droshkies could drive upon it, bringing patrons to buy. He had probably watched from his father's shoulder on that June day in 1814, when Tsar Alexander I, England's ally, had ridden through Camberwell in a gold coach on his state visit to London; now, in this vast and snowy land, he watched Tsar Nicholas I preside at the ancient ceremony of the "breaking of the waters," when the sun finally broke the ice and sent the waters of the Neva roaring down to the sea. To the booming of the cannon, the governor of the province dipped a jeweled goblet into the river and presented it to the tsar. The floating bridges which connected the three parts of the city were swung into place; boatmen thronged the docks to get their cargoes loaded and vessels launched, and for three nights in palace and streets there was feasting and dancing as St. Petersburg celebrated. There is hardly an adequate phrase to express the passionate joy of the true Russian for the advent of spring. It is contagious. And, though his letters from this period were destroyed, it is safe to say that Robert Browning enjoyed every moment of that event, since he never failed to enjoy himself wherever he was.

His secretarial duties were not too demanding. He had time to visit the Hermitage Museum with its magnificent collection of Renaissance paintings, which seems to have made a greater impression upon him than Russian literature. Pushkin's *Eugene Onegin,* which had been published the preceding year, was the talk of St. Petersburg; and since French, in which Browning was fluent, was the language of the upper classes, he could have read the book in translation, and must certainly have heard it discussed along with *Boris Goudenov,* which had taken Russia by storm in 1825; but he mentions neither. However, both "Johannes Agricola in Meditation" and "Porphyria's Lover" are supposed to have been written during his visit to St. Petersburg; their tone of madness mingled with an undertone of melancholy was perhaps inspired by his personal observation of the Slavic temperament. Certainly he must have received an account of the Decembrist Uprising of 1825, and of the incessant peasant revolts, and have heard about the young revolutionary, Mikail Bakunin, who had fled to Switzerland to avoid certain arrest by the secret police, but, perhaps because of his diplomatic connection, he could not comment. He was profoundly moved by Russian music, however, especially the folk songs, and some of them made such a deep impression that he could remember them in the completely different environment of Paris. He astounded Prince Gargarin, fifty years later, by recalling to His Highness words and melodies which the prince himself, native born and bred, had forgotten.

In a word, Browning presumably adapted himself to his new surroundings with enthusiasm and enjoyed his visit. In fact, he almost decided that diplomacy was the life for him, and, had his application for a post in Persia been approved, he might never again have seriously put pen to paper except for Foreign Office dispatches. But his further services were declined, so in June he returned to London. The time away had revived his spirits, and even *Pauline* no longer seemed such a fiasco. He once again resolved to dedicate himself to poetry, and this time the resolve was a firm commitment. Meanwhile, casting about for a suitable subject for his next effort, he prepared himself by reading every word of Samuel Johnson's *Dictionary.*

The French revolution of 1830, which had ousted Charles X and brought Louis Philippe to the throne, had caused many Royalist refugees to seek asylum in England. One of their contacts with the underground Royalist forces in France was twenty-seven year old Count Amédée de Ripert-Monclar, who spent his summers in England— ostensibly on vacation, since the English government had recognized the regime of Louis Philippe. He was acquainted with Browning's uncle, Reuben Browning, who was associated with the House of Rothschild in Paris, and in the summer of 1834 he appeared at Camberwell with a warm letter of introduction. Actually the count's real interests lay in literature and history, rather than in politics, and he and Browning immediately became friends. It was through him that Browning became a member of both the *Institut Historique* and the *Societé Francaise de Statique Universelle,* to which few foreigners were elected. And it was Monclar who suggested the subject of the next Browning poem, *Paracelsus.*

Browning was already familiar with the career of Theophrastus Bombast von Hohenstein, "Paracelsus," the learned fifteenth-century German physician, who burned the books of his predecessors and, with some justification, proclaimed himself as the source of all medical knowledge. There were several books about him in his father's library which Browning had long since read, and Dr. Blundell's lectures supplied the medical background. But the thing that fascinated him most about Paracelsus was the man's dedication to knowledge, a dedication that was almost an obsession and denied all human impulses and emotions, even love. As Browning pondered his poem, Paracelsus gradually emerged as the man who seeks for truth according to rigid, scientific principles, but who fails to recognize that inspiration, intuition, and emotion are

valid sources of truth as well. To his friend's concerned re-
monstrance that such a treatment would leave no room to
introduce love—and what was a poem without love?—
Browning asked for patience and for permission to handle
the subject in his own way!

As a foil for Paracelsus, he created the character Aprile,
a poet who seeks only to love—not only in the sense of
loving another human being, but of loving all beauty—and
who rejects knowledge. Aprile, seeking to create solely
from emotion, dies. Paracelsus, realizing that his own rejection of love has left knowledge unfulfilled, wrongly
seeks to find it in sensual pleasures. Meanwhile, his fame
as a scholar is at its peak, but he finds no comfort or satisfaction in the adulation he receives, for he knows that his
worshipers follow him only because he attacks the authorities, and that they will as readily attack him if he ceases
to please, which they do. Finally, on his deathbed, the secret he has sought so long is revealed to him:

> I saw Aprile— my Aprile there!
> And as the poor melodious wretch disburdened
> His heart, and moaned his weakness in my ear,
> I learned my own deep error; love's undoing
> Taught me the worth of love in man's estate,
> And what proportion love should hold with power
> In his right constitution; love preceding
> Power, and with much power, always much more love ...
> I learned this, and supposed the whole was learned . . .
> In my own heart love had not been made wise
> To trace love's faint beginnings in mankind,
> To know even hate is but a mask of love's,
> To see a good in evil, and a hope
> In ill-success; to sympathize, be proud
> Of their half-reasons, faint aspirings, dim
> Struggles for truth, their poorest fallacies,
> Their prejudice and fears and cares and doubts;

All with a touch of nobleness, despite
Their error, upward tending all though weak,
Like plants in mines which never saw the sun,
But dream of him, and guess where he may be,
And do their best to climb and get to him.

His search for truth, knowledge, and love, as he understood them, had not been infused with any compassion for
ignorance; and his personal pride when ignorance attacked
was not enough to sustain him. Now he is a despised out-
cast, deserted by everyone except Festus, the one friend
who loves him and has always warned him that his pride
would be his downfall. But Paracelsus is comforted in the
knowledge that he had done his best insofar as he knew,
and that God is more merciful than men.

If I stoop
Into a dark tremendous sea of cloud,
It is but for a time; I press God's lamp
Close to my breast; its splendor, soon or late,
Will pierce the gloom.

Paracelsus was published on August 15, 1835, and dedicated to Amédée de Ripert-Monclar. Its reception was an
unqualified critical success. Even the less laudatory reviews
admitted the beauty of the poem and the ambitiousness of
its scope. The majority of reviewers praised it wholeheartedly as a brilliant tour de force, both poetically and philo-
sophically. It was also prophetic, for, twenty-four years before Darwin published his *Origin of Species,* Robert
Browning had grasped intuitively the entire scheme of
evolution, and, even more astounding, anticipated the concept postulated in the twentieth century by Teilhard de
Chardin, that all matter in the universe possesses life, and
all life moves inexorably to the supreme creation, Man.

The doors of literary London were now open to Robert
Browning, and on May 26, 1836, he was invited to a sup-

per party in celebration of the opening night of Thomas Talfourd's new tragedy, *Ion*. It was a glittering occasion, for the play had been a huge success. Talfourd was the host; William Charles Macready, who had created the leading role, was guest of honor, and Miss Mitford, the novelist, and Walter Savage Landor, poet and critic, were among the guests who included most of the writers, poets, actors, and artists of the day. All praised *Paracelsus* in most glowing terms. At one point Talfourd rose and lifted his glass to "the youngest poet of England," and a white-haired man across the table stood with the rest and said, "I am proud to drink your health, Mr. Browning." The speaker was William Wordsworth, **dean** of poets, soon to be made poet laureate. And as if this recognition were not enough to make the youngest poet speechless with emotion, as he left the party at dawn Macready took him by the arm and said urgently, "Write me a play, Browning! And keep me from going to America!"

Robert Browning had arrived. He had reached a dizzying peak, from which he surveyed the world with glowing certainty born of hoped-for success. A life of accomplishment lay before him; there was nothing he dared not do, nothing he dared not attempt. He did not know that, like his hero Paracelsus, he would soon descend into his own "dark tremendous sea of cloud."

3

Macready's request did not come to Robert Browning as a complete surprise. Actually, the two men had already met at the home of the Reverend Fox the preceding November. They had immediately liked each other and exchanged visiting cards. A few days later, Browning had sent the actor a copy of *Paracelsus,* which Macready read and commented on in his diary:

> Read *Paracelsus,* a work of great daring, starred with poetry of thought, feeling and diction, but occasionally obscure; the writer can hardly fail to be a leading spirit of his time.[1]

On several occasions he and Browning had been guests at the same dinner parties, and he had invited Browning to a New Year's Eve gathering at his home. Later he had said of him that he looked "more like a youthful poet than any man I ever saw." [2] In February, Browning had called upon him, accompanied by John Forster, the critic, and they had informally discussed the possibility of his doing a play. Macready had been delighted at the prospect.

> It would indeed be some recompense for the miseries, the humiliations, the heart-sickening disgusts which I have endured in my profession, if, by its exercise, I had awakened a spirit of poetry whose influence would elevate, ennoble, and adorn our degraded drama.

he wrote in his diary on February 16, 1836.

The actor's low estimate of the contemporary theater was an accurate one. The great days of Edmund Kean, John Philip Kemble, and Sarah Siddons were over, and Macready was the only actor of their stature who had risen to take their place. He had made his first appearance at the age of seventeen as Romeo, and at twenty-six his interpretation of Richard III had rivaled the great Kean's. By the time he met Robert Browning, he was in the process of achieving his ambition of playing all the great Shakespearean roles, but he was doing so at the expense of his disposition and health. His diary reveals him as a most meticulous artist, who came to the theater in time to eat his dinner in the full armor of Henry V, in order to be completely at home in it on the stage. He studied over his part before every performance, and criticized himself ruthlessly in his diary afterwards. His irascible temper was legendary; he seems to have been constantly at loggerheads with actors and managers, but the sole difficulty was that his standard was invariably far higher than theirs, and they could not, or would not, meet it.

His principal antagonist was Alfred Bunn, manager of Drury Lane Theatre. Bunn was a practical man, who had made his success by knowing what the public wanted and giving it to them. The usual bill at his theatre consisted of a farce for a curtain raiser, then the main piece—a five-act comedy or tragedy—followed by another farce or "spectacle." The evening began at six and ended after midnight, and there was always the distraction caused by the current theatrical policy of selling tickets for half-price after nine o'clock. Macready, who looked on the theatre as a kind of temple with Shakespeare as its god, suffered terribly under such a regime. It was bad enough to have to come on stage after the audience had shrieked with laughter at the farce, and were waiting impatiently for the main piece to be over so that they could laugh at another farce, or be dazzled by a "spectacle"—for example, the entrance of Miss Vincent in *Thalaba the Destroyer,* "in a Burmese chariot drawn by Burmese bulls, and followed by elephants, ostriches, and other zoological accompaniments from the Surrey Gardens." [3] But when Bunn, in April, 1836, had summarily decreed that only the first three acts of *Richard III* would be played, in order to give more time for the spectacle, Macready's rage exploded. He marched into Bunn's office, called him a damned scoundrel, and struck him across the face.

Bunn promptly sued for damages. Macready left Drury Lane and accepted the invitation to play at Covent Garden, the rival theatre, where a cheering audience stopped the show for ten minutes on his opening night in *Macbeth.* After the final curtain, he thanked the audience and publicly expressed his regret for his behavior to Alfred Bunn. Bunn would not accept this apology, the trial proceeded, and Macready was made to pay enormous damages. This financial loss made the success of his Covent Garden engagement imperative; an American tour was the only alternative, and this Macready regarded as a fate worse than death. Hence, his urgent request to Robert Browning on the opening night of *Ion.* He was well aware, too, of the value of good publicity. After the Bunn catastrophe, he needed to insure himself against possible disapproval, and the announcement, "Mr. Macready will appear in a new tragedy by Mr. Robert Browning" would be certain to draw an audience.

Browning was already at work on his new poem, *Sordello,* but Macready's request was too magnificent an opportunity to let slip. Three days later, on May 28, he wrote a note, saying that his present work was almost complete, so that he could be at the actor's disposal on the first of July, and ". . . if before then any subject should suggest itself to you, I will give my whole heart and soul to the writing of a tragedy to be ready the first of November next." [4] He himself already had an idea in mind. He had put *Sordello* aside in March to help John Forster complete a biography of Thomas Wentworth, Earl of Strafford, the friend of King Charles I, whose unshakeable adherence to his royal patron had finally led him to the scaffold. Browning had found Strafford an interesting subject; the intricacies of mind and emotion had already absorbed his attention in *Paracelsus,* and now he became absorbed in political considerations as well. He saw Strafford as a man who fundamentally was a believer in the people's rights, a Parliamentarian, a true liberal, but who was forced by circumstances and his own stubborn loyalty—even when his sovereign deserted him— to act against his own beliefs. Strafford was truly a tragic figure and could be made a role worthy of the great Macready. On the third of August, he notified the actor of his choice of subject, and Macready wrote jubilantly in his diary, ". . . he could not have hit upon one that I could have more readily concurred in." [5]

Certainly no playwright was ever more auspiciously launched, yet from the very outset there was trouble. Browning apparently did not begin work on the play immediately; he was immersed in *Sordello,* and it was not until October 31 that he called on Macready to tell him that the play was finished, by which he probably meant the first draft. On November 19, he appeared with the manuscript, but Act IV was still incomplete. Macready told him to write out a scenario of it, and settled down to read. He was pleased with the script, but a second reading three days later revealed many flaws. The play was lifeless. The poetry in some places was splendid, but the action was confused. Characters said and did things without recognizable motivation. Macready summoned Browning to his study, stated his objections, and told him that, inasmuch as he had contracted to stage Bulwer-Lytton's new play for his next production, there would be time to make corrections in *Strafford*. He made numerous suggestions for revision, which Browning promised to follow. Later they were both to regret that Macready had not immediately rejected the play.

Months of rewriting followed. At the end of March, 1837, Browning brought in the revised manuscript; ". . . he looks very unwell, jaded and thoughtsick," [6] Macready wrote in his diary. The actor read the play that night, and, though filled with misgivings, he presented it the next day to Obaldiston, manager of Covent Garden Theatre. He half-hoped that Obaldiston would reject it, but the manager liked it and agreed to produce it at once. Macready, having now formally committed himself, went into production with a heavy heart. He was so concerned that, without consulting Browning, he called in John Forster to help make further revisions. This was definitely unprofessional, forgivable only because Forster was the biographer of *Strafford* and therefore knew the historical background well. Browning was furious and said so, in no uncertain terms, and Macready had the difficulty of pacifying him, in addition to all his other anxieties.

The play was read to the company and went into rehearsal. More flaws were revealed; more on-the-spot revisions were made, again without consultation, which brought a demand from Browning that the play be withdrawn. Again Macready pacified him, but Browning sold the original manuscript to a publisher and arranged to have it available at the theatre on opening night so that the audience would know what he had actually written.

Helen Faucit, the leading lady, declared that her role was too insignificant. George Vandenhoof, who played Pym, leader of the Parliamentary forces and the second most important role in the play, said that it was hardly worth the trouble. "I strongly fear it will fail—it is not good," [7] Macready mourned in his diary, and on April 23, nine days before the opening, he wrote, "The more I consider the play, the lower my hopes smile upon it; I expect it will be damned—grievously hissed at the end. . . ."

Only the acting could save the play, he decided, but the role of Strafford offered him little scope. The great moment of the real Strafford's life, his plea to the hostile Parliament which won him so much sympathy that Pym demanded his instant execution lest the people rebel, Robert Browning had by-passed completely. Or, what is more likely, this is the scene which Macready had summarily excised *in toto,* calling it "mere feeble rant." The play opened on May 1 to a packed house. Browning described the occasion as a "perfect gallows." Macready and his company acted as though their lives depended on their performances. To everyone's amazement, the play was a resounding success! The critics praised it so highly that even Macready felt reassured and thought that it would have a fairly decent run. But after the fourth performance, George Vandenhoof withdrew from the cast, and since no one else was available to play the role of Pym, *Strafford* had to close.

Browning was greatly distressed and disturbed. For weeks he importuned Macready to revive the play, offering a completely revised script. This Macready declined to do, but, recognizing that the poet was quite an astute critic of any plays but his own, he occasionally invited him to rehearsals and asked for his comments, so the friendship between the two remained unbroken. Through him, Browning met Dickens and Bulwer-Lytton; he was in the actor's dressing room when Alexandre Dumas, on holiday from Paris, came backstage to pay his respects. He found it exciting to move in these glamorous circles and to have the right to call himself a playwright, even though his own play had been so short-lived.

Also, there was *Sordello,* his current "masterpiece," which was to redeem the failure of *Pauline.* In *Pauline* he had tried to set forth how a poet became conscious of his mission, how a poet's soul came into being, but he had been too personally involved to be properly objective. But Sordello, the romantic poet of Mantua, whom he had discovered when Angelo Cerrutti had tutored him in Italian, whose exploits in love and war would add breadth to the central theme and give no critic the opportunity to say that the poem was his own personal story—Sordello would be his perfect mask. He had planned to have the poem ready for publication in the late summer of 1837. But on July 22, his hopes were dashed to the ground. A Mrs. W. Busk, a "poetess" so minor that no autobiographical account of her survives, published her *Plays and Poems* in two volumes. One of her poems had Sordello as its subject.

To make matters worse, Mrs. Busk had also chosen to concentrate on the same aspects of Sordello as Browning had chosen: poetry, love, and war. Browning saw four years of agonizing work—for he had actually begun his *Sordello* in 1833, soon after the *Pauline* fiasco—irretrievably lost. He had two possible choices: to discard the poem completely or to revise it completely. He chose revision, and plunged into the history of the period. The struggle between the Guelphs and the Ghibilines, which had served merely as background to the story, now moved to the fore. Robert struggled as hard as had his rival armies; Harriet Martineau, the novelist, advised him not to try to be both historian and poet, but to "let the poem tell its own tale."[8] He found himself in that most desperate situation known to any artist—he could not finish his work. Suddenly he made a decision. Perhaps his difficulty was that he had no personal, first-hand knowledge of Italy. Perhaps if he could visit Mantua, Goito, Verona, move in the landscape that Sordello had known, the longed-for inspiration would come.

So, on April 13, 1834, Browning boarded the *Norhan Castle*, bound for Trieste. He was the only passenger. Gales and snow bombarded them so that they were a week reaching Devon, but soon the seas grew calmer, and, a week later, he had his first glimpse of Lisbon. There was a storm in the Bay of Biscay, however, which made him seasick. The captain helped him on deck on April 27 when the ship passed Gibralter, so that he might not miss the "Rock," and he experienced for the first time the "burning heat" of the Mediterranean. A week later, Captain Davidson woke him one morning with the news that there was a capsized ship half a mile away. Browning watched at the rail while the sailors lowered a boat, rowed out to the wreck, made her fast with ropes, and towed her towards the *Norham Castle*. Gradually the wreck righted itself and a body fell from it into the sea. Five more were discovered in the hold when a boarding party went to investigate— "don't imagine the wretched state of things,"[9] Browning wrote to a friend in London. As usual, he was right there and missing nothing. The boarding party discovered quantities of cigars and tobacco and bales of cloth in the hold; the ship had evidently been a smuggler bound for Gibralter. Browning took two cutlasses and a sword for souvenirs before Captain Davidson ordered her cut adrift, and he stood watching while she sank: ". . . you can hardly conceive the strange sight when the battered hulk turned

round, actually, and looked at us, and then reeled off." [10]
There was no further excitement after that. The *Norhan Castle* continued placidly along the coast of Africa; Browning enjoyed the scenery and wrote two poems on the fly-leaves of the book he had carried with him—"Home-Thoughts from the Sea," and "How They Brought the Good News from Ghent to Aix."

He reached Trieste on the twentieth of May, and the next evening took the steamer for Venice. He found that city so fascinating that he stayed there for two weeks. Then he went on through Treviso and Bassano, stopped at Asolo, which he described as "delicious," for four days, then on through the mountains via Possagno and Romano d' Ezzelino—places seldom visited, but filled with memories of the great events he was wrestling with in *Sordello*. He returned to Venice via Vicenza and Padua, then traveled through the Tyrol and up the Rhine. He had missed the coronation of Queen Victoria, and he had not added a line to *Sordello*, but he had had one experience which was to alter entirely his concept of his hero. In Venice he had mingled with the crowds celebrating the Corpus Christi carnival. He had watched them throng into the Piazza San Marco, singing and shouting; he had sat on a ruined palace step looking at the gondola procession. It was an exciting scene, gay and colorful, but Browning, in a quick flash of insight, perceived the misery hidden beneath that gaiety.

> There is such niggard stock of happiness
> To share, that, do one's uttermost, dear wretch,
> One labors ineffectually to stretch
> It o'er you, so that mother and children both
> May equitably flaunt the sumpter-cloth.
>
> *Sordello*, Book III

Filled with swift compassion for the "warped souls and bodies" of the people before him, who were trying to find a brief respite from their unhappy lives by frantic merry-making, he found his key to the character of Sordello which had so long eluded him. The poet-lover must have been a man divided against himself, one who longed for greatness as a poet, but was forced by his compassion for suffering humanity to lead men into battle against those who upheld tyranny, even though the tyrants might be the people whom he loved. In *Strafford* Robert Browning had explored the soul of a man whose political loyalties had forced him to go against his instinct; the battle of a man forced to choose between his liberal beliefs and creative powers would be a splendid follow-up. "You will see *Sordello* in a trice, if the fagging fit holds," [11] he wrote to Fanny Hayworth on July 31, a few days after his arrival in London.

But no one saw *Sordello* in a trice, including Browning. He was still bitten by the theatre bug, and had for some months been meditating, along with his major work, on another tragedy for Macready. Another historical theme had awakened his interest: the story of Victor, King of Sardinia, a tyrant, who abdicated in order to marry a commoner and gave his crown to his son, Charles, a seemingly diffident, malleable young man whom his father expected to direct behind the scenes. But Charles took on courage and determination with his coronation robes and refused to be manipulated. King Victor demanded his crown again, raised a rebellion, and was taken prisoner; he was confined in the castle at Rivoli until his death two years later. Browning, as might be expected, considering the current bent of his own mind, quite unhistorically endowed Charles with a very liberal and humanitarian point-of-view, in contrast to his father's harshness. The first draft of the play *King Victor and King Charles* may have been written immediately upon his return from Italy, for the character of Charles reads rather like a rehearsal for the

Sordello who finally emerged in the last version of the long poem.

He was occupied with *Sordello* during the entire winter, verifying the material he had obtained in Italy, strengthening—as he thought—the growth of his hero's liberal sympathies, and writing the dramatic climax where Sordello, confronted with the choice between taking the crown he is entitled to by birth, and being the leader of the people's cause, tears off the emperor's badge, tramples it underfoot and dies, worn out by his emotional conflicts. The poem was finished in May, 1839. Browning had expended six years on it. He was certain that it would be a triumph for him; the critics, and the public too, waited its publication with great anticipation.

Sordello appeared on February 24, 1840, two weeks after Queen Victoria's wedding to Prince Albert of Saxe-Coburg-Gotha. The expenses of publication were paid by the poet's father. Browning's tension grew as he waited for the reviews. He had, just a few weeks earlier, submitted his play, *King Victor and King Charles,* to Macready, who rejected it out of hand. In fact, Macready called it "a great mistake." [12] Browning, smarting under this disparagement, was all the more eager for *Sordello's* unqualified success to vindicate himself. He was completely unprepared for the torrent of adverse criticism that, without exception, was leveled at both poem and poet. The reviewers were unanimous in their bewilderment and their annoyance. The *Spectator* said that the poem was filled with "digression, affectation, obscurity, and all the faults that spring, it would seem, from crudity of plan and self opinion." The *Athenæum* declared it "mannered, obscure, harsh, and full of platitudes." Another review dismissed it as showing all the poet's worst faults and none of his virtues.

Even his friends disliked it. Miss Martineau said that she was so bewildered by the poem, she thought she must be ill. Mrs. Thomas Carlyle, who had fully comprehended her husband's quite chaotic *Sartor Resartus,* said that she had read *Sordello* unable to determine whether the subject was a man, or a city, or a book. This rather malicious remark could be dismissed as prejudice, for Jane Welsh Carlyle was not especially fond of Robert Browning, but other persons upon whose good opinion he had depended, felt much the same. *Sordello* achieved then and there the reputation of being the most obscure and unintelligible poem in the English language.

Browning, for his part, was both bewildered and resentful, and inclined to blame the public for its lack of comprehension. The words of Naddo, the old poet, to the young Sordello,

> The knowledge that you are a bard
> Must constitute your prime, nay, sole reward!

must often have been in his mind during those months following publication. He could not see the poem's obvious fault: that in permitting the youthful poet-lover to be superceded by Sordello, champion of the people, he had not only made romance give way to history, but, even worse, had turned history into histrionics and poetry into political argument. Also, he had credited his readers with the same knowledge of the Guelph and Ghibiline struggle that years of research had made his own. Much of the obscurity of the poem rises from the lack of much-needed explanations. Many years later Browning revised *Sordello,* adding marginal glosses, but even these could not erase the poem's fundamental weakness—its hero's complete lack of motivation. Perhaps the fault lay within Browning himself; perhaps, despite the time and effort he had expended or even because of them, he had not thought carefully and deeply enough to make Sordello's conversion from creative genius to man of action ring true.

The most regrettable thing about the poem was that it ruined the reputation that *Paracelsus* had gained for him. To the end of his life, Robert Browning was identified as the poet of *Sordello,* and *Sordello* may have been one reason why critics were so willing to find obscurity in his later works. As T. R. Lounsbury wrote in 1911, "It [*Sordello*] is a colossal derelict on the sea of literature, inflicting damage on the strongest intellects that graze it even slightly, and hopelessly wrecking the frailer craft that come into full collision with it. . . ." [13] and this opinion certainly sums up the critical reaction of 1840 as well. Browning was really crushed by the indictment. The debacle of *Pauline* was a minor upheaval, compared to this cataclysm.

But, though he did not then know it, the first step in remaking his reputation had already been taken. During his trip to Italy, he had visited the little town of Asolo and fallen in love with it. One day in the early spring of 1838, he had gone for a walk in Dulwich Woods as a respite from *Sordello,* when an idea flashed across his mind—how an obscure person, walking alone through the world, might have an influence on people and events entirely unknown to himself. Asolo and Dulwich Woods merged, and gradually he had created the little silk winder, Pippa. The fleeting thought grew into *Pippa Passes,* which he wrote as soon as *Sordello* had gone to press, and sent it to his publisher, Edward Moxon. It was a simple story of a child who had but one holiday a year and spent it walking and singing in the hills, and Browning considered it a mere trifle, compared to the complex and weighty *Sordello.* Nevertheless, he liked it, and so did Moxon, who promptly accepted it. *Sordello* had taken six years to complete; *Pippa Passes* was written in as many weeks, but it was to have far-reaching consequences, more important than Browning could have envisioned in his wildest dreams.

4

Edward Moxon of Dover Street was a most unusual man. He had begun his career at the age of nine, as an apprentice to a bookseller in his native Wakefield, the town made famous by Oliver Goldsmith's novel; twenty years later he was established as a publisher in London. He had the excellent taste and great good fortune to publish a volume of Charles Lamb's verses and, further, to marry Lamb's adopted daughter, Emma Isola. He lacked formal education, but his own omniverous reading had given him a cultural background sufficient to make him a welcome guest at Samuel Rogers' celebrated literary breakfasts, where the guest list was decidedly interesting and limited. It was he, also, who published Tennyson's first volume in 1832, which had drawn critical barbs, but his "discovery" of a new poet paid valuable dividends when Tennyson became poet laureate in 1850. In 1834, Moxon received what amounted to an accolade: permission from Wordsworth to publish the definitive edition of his works. Soon afterwards he added the names of Benjamin Disraeli and Walter Savage Landor to his list. Nor were the traditional authors neglected: Moxon eventually published new editions of Chaucer, Dryden, Shakespeare and Spenser; but already, in 1840, his was a position of considerable prestige in the publishing world.

He had been one of the several publishers who had rejected Browning's *Paracelsus*. That rejection had been a mistake, which, as a practical man of business, he decided to rectify by the publication of *Sordello*. The failure of *Sordello* might have daunted a less intrepid man, but

Moxon continued to have faith in Robert Browning. He suggested a scheme by which Browning's future work could be published and distributed at minimum cost; his faith did not extend to financial backing, which the poet would have to provide for himself. Small paperback pamphlets would be inexpensive to print, however, and could be sold at a shilling, a price which almost any reader could afford.

Browning concurred with the scheme enthusiastically. True, pamphlets were not as distinguished as an octavo volume, but they might reach a wider audience. He discussed the project with his father, who agreed to pay the costs of publication for what Browning had already decided would be a *series* of pamphlets, devoted exclusively to his plays. Macready's rejection of *King Victor and King Charles* still rankled, and he had hope of its better acceptance by the reading public. He had another play in hand as well—*The Return of the Druses*—and these, with *Pippa Passes*, would make an excellent beginning for the series. He chose as its general title *Bells and Pomegranates*, using as source the passage from the twenty-eighth chapter of Exodus, where the high priest's robe is described:

> And beneath upon the hem of it thou shalt make pomegranates of blue, and of purple, and of scarlet, round about the hem thereof; and bells of gold between them round about.

The title, as he later explained, was symbolic, intending to convey that his poetry was "an alteration, or mixture, of music with discoursing, sound with sense, poetry with thought." [1] A very personal interpretation, which thoroughly eluded both critics and readers, and further increased the reputation for obscurity which he had acquired in *Sordello*.

Pippa Passes was scheduled for publication in the spring of 1840, to capitalize on the anticipated success of *Sordello*. That fiasco made Moxon decide to delay the new book; it is also possible that the day was lengthened because of the lawsuit which was filed against him that autumn for publishing "blasphemous, libelous books," the complainant's description of the complete edition of Shelley's poems edited by Mary Godwin Shelley, the poet's widow! The trial was highly publicized; Thomas Talfourd, who was a very able barrister as well as a popular playwright, defended Moxon, thus making the occasion an extremely literary one. The judgment went against Moxon, but no fine was imposed, and the edition of Shelley went forward as planned. The publisher could then turn his attention to the rest of his list, and in April, 1841, *Pippa Passes* appeared in the bookstores. The title page carried the name, "Robert Browning, author of *Paracelsus*." Significantly, *Sordello* not mentioned.

Pippa Passes was very coolly received. Only John Forster, who had constituted himself Robert Browning's critical defender, gave it kindly mention, saying that the poet seemed to be on the right road at last. Strangely enough, though the poem's theme should certainly have appealed to the sentimentality of the age, and the current Parliamentary investigation of child labor conditions made it a very timely one, the reading public was slow to discover *Pippa Passes*. It took nearly twenty years for Pippa to find her place among the great poetic creations of the Victorian age. In the twentieth century, the poem occupies a pre-eminent place in the Browning canon. Pippa's songs, especially the first—

> The year's at the spring
> The day's at the morn;
> Morning's at seven;

> The hillside dew-pearled;
> The lark's on the wing;
> The snail's on the thorn;
> God's in his Heaven—
> All's right with the world!

are regularly included in all anthologies. Her innocence
and charm can still arouse sympathy even in a cynical
age, and the irony implicit in her imagining the happy
lives of those who live in the houses she passes—for the
reader knows, as she does not, that the people in them are
far from happy—is beautifully evoked. If the idea that her
songs could move a pair of guilty lovers to repentance,
heal a broken marriage, avert a political conspiracy, and
save her own life, seems naïveté on her creator's part, and
the songs themselves merely a poetical device, the essential
truth of the poet's premise remains:

> All service ranks the same with God:
> If now, as formerly he trod
> Paradise, his presence fills
> Our earth, each only as God wills
> Can work—God's puppets, best and worst,
> Are we; there is no last or first.
>
> Say not "a small event!" Why "small"?
> Costs it more pain than this, ye call
> A "great event," should come to pass,
> Than that? Untwine me from the mass
> Of deeds which make up life, one deed
> Power shall fall short in or exceed!

Pippa herself is a lovely, appealing figure, alive and be-
lievable in her irresistible joy and her gratitude for life
despite its harshness. Her song has been set to music, and is
sung all over the world to this day. Robert Browning loved
Pippa Passes; he wrote to Elizabeth Barrett during their

courtship, "And when I say that I like 'Pippa' better than anything else I have done, I shall have answered all you bade me." [2] *Pippa Passes* was the one work which Elizabeth Barrett wistfully admitted that she wished she might have written.

The second number of *Bells and Pomegranates,* the play *King Victor and King Charles,* appeared in 1842, again to critical oblivion. John Forster barely mentioned it, saying that it showed signs of better poetry. It is possible that Macready's rejection, which he and Browning had doubtless discussed with their respective friends, for neither of them was at all reticent about expressing his opinion, prejudiced even those readers who might have bought copies in spite of it. It was an unlucky work from the start, and even at a shilling a copy it was a failure. Browning was not daunted. He was still determined to find an audience for his plays, even though Macready had, by this time, also summarily rejected his latest effort, *The Return of the Druses;* and he proposed that play to Moxon as *Bells and Pomegranates III.*

Moxon demurred. He felt that to publish a third play after two failures would be imprudent. He suggested a collection of short poems, "for popularity's sake," [3] as Browning wrote rather scornfully to Alfred Domett. But Moxon was a business man, after all, and business had been very poor. The Afghan War was raging, and the papers had been filled for months with stories of atrocities committed against the British residents of Kabul, climaxed by the massacre of an entire British regiment at the Khyber Pass by the fanatic troops of Dost Mohammed, the Afghan ruler. People simply were not in the mood for anything too demanding, so Browning agreed to this change of pace, and *Bells and Pomegranates III: Dramatic Lyrics,* was published in November, 1842. Again, Forster

45

was the only critic to pay any attention to it. "Mr. Browning is a genuine poet, and only needs to have less misgiving on the subject himself," he wrote in the *Examiner* on November 25. He especially liked "The Pied Piper," which Browning had written to entertain Macready's son, and which has continued to attract adults as well as children for over a hundred years. He also approved of "Incident of the French Camp." He said nothing about "Johannes Agricola" or "Porphyria's Lover," perhaps because both had been previously published in the *Monthly Repository*. But the most striking ommissions in his critique were "My Last Duchess" and "Soliloquy of the Spanish Cloister," both now acknowledged as among Robert Browning's greatest dramatic monologues, the form which he was ultimately to make his own superb poetic medium.

Browning himself seems to have been unaware that he had found his métier at last, for in November, 1842, he was still trying to be a playwright and was engaged in a battle royal with Macready over his new tragedy, *A Blot in the 'Scutcheon*. He had finished the play in December, 1840, and sent it to Macready, but at that time the actor had been heavily involved in taking over the management of Drury Lane and had laid the manuscript aside. He did not read it until September, 1841, and then only at John Forster's insistence. He made no mention of the play in his diary, indicating, perhaps, that the opinion he had recorded about *The Return of the Druses*—that Browning would never write again to any purpose—still held. He did mention seeing the poet on several occasions during the winter of 1841–42; once they went together to call on Charles Dickens, and at least twice they were guests at the same dinner parties, but they evidently did not discuss the new play. The diary mentions "a note from Browning" on March 4, 1842, and a quite pointed letter, probably

One of the earliest known portraits of Robert Browning. Original drawing by Count Amedée de Ripert Monclar.
The Prints Division, The New York Public Library.

Elizabeth Barrett Browning.
The Picture Collection, The New York Public Library.

50 Wimpole Street, London, where Elizabeth Barrett lived while being courted by Robert Browning.
The Prints Division, The New York Public Library.

written in April, makes clear Browning's annoyance at the delay:

> I have forborne troubling you about my Play from a conviction that you would do the very best possible for us both in the matter: but as the Season is drawing (I suppose) to an end, and no piece is at present announced in the bills, it has struck me that in all likelihood the failure of *Plighted Troth* may render it inexpedient, in your opinion, to venture on a fresh trial in this Campaign, and I stand, if I remember rightly, next in Succession on your list.[4]

Actually, *A Blot in the 'Scutcheon* should have preceded the dismal *Plighted Troth,* a tragedy by the Reverend C. F. Darly which had closed after one performance, because it had been in the actor's hands for months before the other had been submitted, as both Macready and Browning were well aware. Browning was further distressed that the actor's procrastination had delayed his own plans:

> . . . that quiet, generally intelligible, and (for me!) popular sort of thing was to have been my *second number* of plays—on your being gracious to it, I delayed issuing any further attempts for a year—and now have published a very indifferent substitute [*King Victor and King Charles*]. . . .[5]

He requested Macready to return the play so that he might publish it.

Macready replied a week later, expressing his regrets, and on May 22 invited Browning to a party at his home. Four days later he left for a month's tour of Ireland, returning to London at the end of June. On July 14, Browning wrote again; but Macready, harassed by the

47

many problems of being an actor-manager, and in deep financial straits because Drury Lane was costing him all his savings, decided to produce Westland Marston's *The Patrician's Daughter* as his first new play of the 1842–43 season. It is unfortunate that so much of the correspondence between the actor and poet was destroyed, for it must have been extensive, and would, perhaps, throw light on a rather astonishing episode of October 13, 1842, when Browning sent back his card to Macready after a performance, and Macready declined to receive him. Browning's note, written a few days later, has survived; in it he apologized for being "unwittingly . . . singularly intrusive in the past,"[6] indicating that relations between the two were strained.

At some point between September, 1841, and November, 1842, John Forster took it upon himself to send *A Blot in the 'Scutcheon* to Charles Dickens for his opinion. On November 25, Dickens returned his verdict in a letter to Forster:

> Browning's play has thrown me into a perfect passion of sorrow. To say that there is anything in its subject save what is lovely, true, deeply affecting, full of the best emotion, the most earnest feeling, and the most true and tender source of interest, is to say that there is no light in the sun and no heat in the blood. It is full of genius, natural and great thoughts, profound and yet simple and beautiful in its vigour . . . And I swear it is a tragedy that *must* be played; and must be played, moreover, by Macready. . . .[7]

Dicken's enthusiasm turned the tide. Macready summoned

Browning on the thirteenth of December, and told him that he would produce the play.

Meanwhile, *The Return of the Druses* was being readied for publication and appeared in January, 1843, as *Bells and Pomegranates IV*. The play concerned a Lebanese warrior, Djabal, member of the Druse sect, who pretended to be the reincarnation of his people's divinized hero in order to deliver them from bondage; but his conscience will not allow him to live a lie indefinitely and, torn with remorse, he kills himself. The critics ignored *The Return of the Druses* unanimously; even John Forster could not find a word to say in its favor.

Nor was Robert Browning permitted to recover from this blow to his self-esteem. He had liked the play, thought the role of Djabal made to order for Macready, and had counted upon the reading public to vindicate him. Instead, the public had upheld Macready, and Macready's unconcealed satisfaction was difficult to bear, especially when every possible misfortune was dogging *A Blot in the 'Scutcheon,* which had gone into rehearsal in January, 1843. To begin with, the plot of the play was completely incredible. A young man who fears to ask his beloved's brother for her hand, and yet permits his beloved to drift into a clandestine affair, is not precisely an heroic figure; and a young girl who is expecting a child, and then refuses because of her remorse for her sin to marry the man responsible when he does finally get up enough courage to ask her brother, is pathetic, but hardly tragic. Tresham, the brother, whose pride is so great that he considers a blot upon the family escutcheon a fate worse than death, is unsympathetic in the extreme. Macready struggled valiantly with the play, cutting and revising over Browning's heated objections, but he hated the role of Tresham. After a few days he decided to abandon it to Samuel Phelps, another member of the company, unless Browning would permit him to postpone production until after Easter.

Browning declined postponement and declared himself perfectly satisfied with Mr. Phelps in the role. In this, he later admitted, he was both stubborn and stupid, for the play needed an actor of Macready's calibre, which Phelps, though competent, was not. Macready foresaw disaster, and, when Phelps became unexpectedly ill, he put aside his personal feeling for the sake of his theatre, and resumed the part. But Phelps refused to resign the role and Brownnig stood with him. Macready was furious. "I could only think Mr. Browning a very disagreeable and offensively mannered person," he wrote in his diary on February 10. Now he did everything possible to negate the success of the play; Browning's friend, Joseph Arnold, wrote about Macready's childishness to Alfred Domett:

> You can imagine the fury and whirlwind of our
> managerial wrath—silent fury, a compressed
> whirlwind, volcano fires burning white in our pent
> heart. We say nothing, of course, but we do our
> spiteful uttermost; we give no orders—we provide
> paltry machinery—we issue mandates to all our
> independent pen-wielders—to all tribes of men who
> rejoice in suppers and distinguished society. Under
> the penalty of our managerial frown, they are to be
> up and doing in their dirty work.[8]

The play ran for three performances; the galleries were packed, but the boxes were empty. Social London would not come to see a new play at Drury Lane unless Macready was on stage. Browning took very small satisfaction in the fact that the play was published as *Bells and Pomegranates*

V on February 11, 1843, and was therefore available for sale in the lobby at the opening performance.

A Blot in the 'Scutcheon marked the end of the friendship between the poet and the actor for many years. Thereafter they met seldom; ". . . saw Browning, who did not speak to me—the *puppy!*" Macready wrote in his diary in June, 1846, and he never spoke of Browning's poetry without disparagement. The breach persisted for over twenty years, until the death of Macready's wife, when Browning wrote a letter of condolence to him, and the two men, in mellower moods, resumed their former pleasant relationship. "I found Macready as I left him—and happily after a long interval resumed him," [9] Browning wrote of that occasion the year before his death and he added a most generous and perceptive portrait of the actor:

> He was one of the most admirable, and, indeed, fascinating characters I have ever known: somewhat too sensitive for his own happiness, and much too impulsive for invariable consistency with his nobler moods.[10]

A Blot in the 'Scutcheon did, however, bring Robert Browning to the attention of Charles Kean, son of the great Edmund Kean, who was now manager of Covent Garden Theatre, and he commissioned Browning to write a play for him. In March, 1844, Browning brought him the script of *Colombe's Birthday*. Kean was an enormously popular actor-manager, chiefly noted for his productions of Shakespeare which were authentic down to the last historical detail, and the Covent Garden seasons were booked for the next three years. He offered to do the play in 1847, provided it remained unpublished, but Browning, eager to get on with the *Bells and Pomegranates* series, would not agree. *Colombe's Birthday* was published in April, 1844, to the critical disinterest which was becoming habitual for any work by Robert Browning.

In autumn of that year, Browning decided to make another journey to Italy. He was worn out by the Macready fracas, and he felt that he needed a change of scene. He sailed to Naples, then went on to visit Rome for the first time. Here he paid his respects at the grave of Shelley and wandered by chance into St. Praxed's Church. Then he traveled to Leghorn, where he called upon Edward Trelawny, whom he was most anxious to meet, for Trelawny had been a friend of Byron and Shelley, and had been the last person to see the "sun-treader" before his death. Certainly the fifty-two year old adventurer and the young poet must have had much to say to each other before Browning left Italy in November and returned to London.

When he arrived home, he found that a friend, John Kenyon, had sent his sister, Sariana, a volume by a new poet named Elizabeth Barrett, which had been widely praised. One of Robert Browning's sincerest and most delightful characteristics was his immediate, sympathetic interest in the work of his contemporaries. Another man might have been jealous at the critical acclaim of another poet, and a woman at that, but he was not. He sat down almost immediately to read the book, and his enthusiasm grew with every page. Then, he came to the poem "Lady Geraldine's Courtship," and the passage where the heroine's suitor reads aloud from Spenser, Wordsworth, Tennyson,

> Or from some Browning some "pomegranet" which if cut down the middle,
> Shows a heart within blood tinctured, of a veined humanity.

Browning's reticence about his personal emotions was great. He kept no soul-searching diary and never consciously revealed himself in his poetry; he had withdrawn *Pauline* because it had given too much unconscious self-revelation. But seeing himself referred to in this manner by another poet, in print, must have stirred him. Someone at last had noticed him, and his appreciation for Miss Barrett's opinion doubtless increased his pleasure in her poetry! His delight in this public recognition must have been considerable. Also, it came at a quite crucial moment in his life, in that he was thirty-two years old, and had never been seriously in love. He later confessed to a kind of "male prudery in respect to young ladies"; in accordance with the conventions of his time, he had been taught to reverence, even idolize women, and the few women he had known well—his mother and the Flower sisters—were the kind who certainly deserved their pedestals. There had been a few brief "attachments," to use the Victorian word, for he was a very attractive, eligible young man. But he was not the sort, evidently, who could be long attracted by the vapid insipidity that most young girls he had met affected. It needed a mind to match, or at least to complement, his own to hold his interest beyond an hour or so of mild flirtation.

Did the thought that Elizabeth Barrett might be the one he had been unconsciously seeking come to him in a sudden flash of intuition? It is possible. He had experienced such a moment in Kean's performance in 1832. It is certain that by 1844, his own mind and creative spirit, which had for ten years been exploring and proclaiming the need of love in a man's life to balance whatever intellect he possessed, were attuned to such a revelation. But he did not act precipitously. Not about this. Notwithstanding his impatience, since there was more than one "dark tremendous sea of cloud" to descend into, he made discreet, even shy inquiry here and there, and conferred with John Kenyon, who was, he discovered, Elizabeth Barrett's distant cousin, as to whether he might with propriety write a letter of congratulations to the lady. Only upon being assured that Miss Barrett would surely be pleased to receive such a letter, did he write on January 10, 1845, "I love your verses with all my heart, dear Miss Barrett." And then, sea of cloud to the contrary, he added boldly, impulsively, "and I love you, too."

5

The courtship of Robert Browning and Elizabeth Barrett has gone down in history as one of the greatest love stories of all time. Certainly from the start it had all the elements of romance: a frail, invalid heroine kept in virtual imprisonment by a stern, unyielding father; a gallant hero determined to rescue her; a secret wedding; a dramatic flight to Italy where the lovers find their joy in a perfect marriage. It is easy to sentimentalize this climactic period in the lives of the two poets, and fiction, theatre, and Hollywood have all done their share. Maudlin sentimentality, however, is incompatible with two such vital, sensitive, but fundamentally sensible people. Romantic, they were all their lives; unintelligently sentimental, never. Besides everything else, they were both blessed with abundant senses of humor.

Elizabeth Barrett was an invalid—so much is true. For three years before meeting Robert Browning, she had lived in an almost hermetically sealed room on the second floor of a gloomy house at 50 Wimpole Street. But, though this was not recognized in the 1840's, her invalidism was as much emotional as physical. The diagnosis of emotionally induced illness is a comparatively new medical discovery, of which Elizabeth's physicians knew nothing. The only remedies that they could prescribe were opium or morphine to dull physical pain, and seclusion to ensure that the patient was not unduly excited. Seclusion Elizabeth most certainly had. Even her own family she saw only at stated intervals, and then usually one member at a time. Her father came in once a day, after dinner, to pray with her and give her her prescribed dose. Apart from them and her faithful maid Wilson—and a cocker spaniel named Flush—she saw no one, except her cousin John Kenyon, and two novelists, Miss Mitford and Mrs. Jameson, whose visits were also strictly limited.

It had not always been so. In her childhood she had been known as a vivacious little girl, quite pretty, somewhat delicate, but not extraordinarily frail. Victorian girls were supposed to be "delicate." Born in 1806, the eldest child of a family of eleven children, she had spent the first twenty-six years of her life in comfortable, even opulent, surroundings. Her father, Edward Moulton Barrett, came from a family of wealthy Jamaican planters, so he was able to afford a beautiful home—"Hope End" estate in the Malvern Hills—and to give his sons and daughters every advantage. Elizabeth was extremely precocious; she insisted upon learning Greek and Latin along with her brothers, and, in 1820, at the age of fourteen, she wrote an epic poem entitled "The Battle of Marathon." Her parents were very proud of it and had copies printed for distribution to friends. Her first public appearance came in the following year, when two of her short poems were published anonymously in the *New Monthly Magazine*. These were followed by "Stanzas on the Death of Lord Byron" in 1824; in 1826, her long philosophical poem, "An Essay on Mind," was published in London (again anoymously) and noted by several critical reviews. Their remarks were not altogether favorable, but Elizabeth only treasured the more her father's comment that the preface would do honor to any man.

She was twenty-two when tragedy touched her for the first time. Her mother had been in poor health for several months, and the family doctor prescribed a stay at Cheltenham where the climate was milder. Within two weeks after her departure from "Hope End," she was dead. Elizabeth had always been very close to her mother, and she was nearly prostrated with grief compounded with guilt because she had not gone to Cheltenham with her. She was also racked by the strange fear that she had loved her mother too much and God not enough. The "jealous God" of evangelical Victorian piety had a strong hold upon her.

No sooner had she recovered to some extent from the stunning impact of this loss and grief, when a second blow fell. Her father's Jamaican interests had been failing. As was typical of the nineteenth century father, he had not confided this fact to anyone, least of all to his eldest daughter. "Females" were sheltered from the affairs of the world and were, therefore, all the more overwhelmed when financial disaster came. Several years passed in litigation, during which Elizabeth agonized over the rumors and gossip that reached her and about which she dared not question her father, but in 1831 Mr. Barrett was obliged to own defeat. "Hope End" was put up for sale to satisfy his creditors, and Elizabeth had to endure the sight of prospective buyers trooping through the home she loved, many of whom took no pains to conceal their gloating at the fall of the Barrett fortunes. It was at this time that her father finally assumed the determined, arrogant shell which successfully masked whatever sympathy or gentleness he had ever possessed—which, admittedly, was not much!

The family moved to Sidmouth, then to London, finally taking up residence at Wimpole Street in the autumn of 1837. Elizabeth, understandably sensitive about her circumstances, for financial failure was considered a great disgrace, found her consolation in work. She studied Hebrew, read philosophy, religious works, and French novels. She also continued to write, and in June, 1838, the first volume published under her name, *The Seraphim and Other Poems,* was advertised in the *Times.* It was enthusiastically received, and, within a few months, Elizabeth was hailed as the most promising of all the younger poets. True, the reviews also mentioned her faults—the lushness of her descriptions, her over-use of adjectives, her faulty rhymes and meters, her inability to sustain a mood. But there was a freshness and sincerity in her work which raised her above the innumerable "poetesses" of the time to the rank of poet. Richard Henry Horne, one of the most astute critics of the day, comparing her to Caroline Norton (a "poetess" now forgotten), said that Miss Norton was "all womanhood," but that Miss Barrett was "all wings."

She was not permitted to enjoy her success long. That summer her health declined alarmingly after a blood vessel ruptured in one of her lungs. Tuberculosis was feared, and her doctor prescribed a warmer climate. Mr. Barrett objected strenuously. The financial problem did not enter here; Elizabeth had inherited a small income from her mother's estate which had been saved from the family wreckage. But she could not travel alone with safety, or, according to the conventions, with propriety, and Mr. Barrett did not wish to have his family divided. He was overruled, however, and in August, 1838, Elizabeth, her sister Henrietta, and her brothers, George and Edward, went by ship and packet boat to Torquay on the Devonshire coast.

At first her health seemed to improve, but in January, 1839, she had a serious relapse, and it was decided that she must remain at Torquay indefinitely. Mr. Barrett was annoyed, but he gave permission. She was ordered not to read or to write, but to deny herself these two joys of her life was quite impossible. She read Plato and wrote a number of poems which were accepted in the magazines. Gradually the congestion in her lungs abated, though she was greatly dependent upon an opium and brandy mixture to quiet her nerves. She had been at Torquay for eighteen months, when the tragedy occurred which drove her to the verge of complete nervous collapse.

Since her mother's death, her brother Edward, whom she called "Bro," had become her closest companion and confidante. On a Saturday in July, 1840, he went sailing with two of his friends. A squall came up and the boat capsized. For three days Elizabeth watched and waited, torn by agonies of remorse, for "Bro" had remained with her over their father's strongly expressed objections. She kept thinking to herself, *"You* have done this." Finally her brother's body was washed ashore. Prostrate with grief and guilt, Elizabeth became hysterical and finally delirious. Only morphine could quiet her. For nearly three months, Henrietta and her other sister Arabel who had come to join her, nursed her, comforted her, wept with her, and gravely feared that there would be a second burial in the churchyard at Torquay.

Slowly she emerged from shock; slowly she began to regain a little strength. Her father ordered her home, but her doctor refused permission. For months she had to be lifted from her bed to her couch and back again; the slightest exertion made her weak, and any attempt to walk brought on a fainting spell. She had to remain at Torquay until September, 1841; then, as she put it wryly, "Poor papa's domestic peace" had to be restored, and she began the journey back to London, lying on a bed in a carriage suspended on a thousand springs. Once the doors of 50 Wimpole Street closed behind her, she determined never to set foot out of her room again. Papa, now that she had returned, no longer thundered, and, as long as she remained an invalid, everyone's domestic peace was ensured.

But her literary life continued. She wrote and published and read. She had read *Paracelsus* within a few weeks of its publication—her cousin Kenyon had sent her a copy—and had been enthralled by it. She had even praised *Sordello,* calling it a "great painting with its face, alas, turned to the wall." She had told Miss Mitford that Robert Browning was "a poet in the holy sense," and had been irritated when Miss Mitford had not agreed. So Browning's letter of congratulation really thrilled her. "I had a letter from Browning the poet last night," she wrote to Mrs. Martin, an old friend of the "Hope End" days, "which threw me into ecstasies—Browning, the author of *Paracelsus* and the king of mystics!" [1] Her reply to Robert Browning, written on the same day, was rather more circumspect:

> I thank you, dear Mr. Browning, from the bottom of my heart. You meant to give me pleasure by your letter, and even if the object had not been answered, I ought still to thank you. But it is thoroughly answered. Such a letter from such a hand! Sympathy is dear—very dear to me: but the sympathy of a poet, and of such a poet, is the quintessence of sympathy to me! Will you take my gratitude for it? [2]

She concluded, "I am proud to remain your obliged and faithful Elizabeth Barrett."

In that same letter, however, she also tentatively suggested that she would be grateful for any criticism he might offer of her work, and Browning was quick to take advantage of the opportunity to continue the correspondence. Two days later he wrote that he really had no criticism to make.

> . . . your poetry must be, cannot but be, infinitely more to me than mine to you—for you *do* what I always wanted, hoped to do, and only seem now likely

to do for the first time. You speak out, *you*—I make only men and women speak.[3]

He mentioned in passing that he was engaged on a new work. Elizabeth quickly replied that she heard this with delight and asked if she might know of its progress.

A relationship which began with an exchange of compliments quickly deepened to one of exchange of mutual confidences. The first few months found them writing to each other once a week or oftener. Elizabeth, deprived of the sympathy and understanding which her mother and "Bro" had given her, found Browning an ideal correspondent, for he understood her dreams and aspirations and did not laugh at them. And she fully understood and sympathized with his. They discussed their own work, literature in general, translated passages of Aeschylus for each other, and exchanged childhood reminiscences. By February, 1845, Browning had begun his patient importuning for permission to call: ". . . in Spring I shall see you, surely see you—for when did I once fail to get whatever I set my heart upon?"[4] In March, his urgency increased. "Do you think I shall see you in two months, three months?"[5]

Elizabeth alternately encouraged his hopes and withdrew that encouragement. She knew that she was already enormously attracted by Robert Browning, but she was also afraid—afraid that he would be disappointed by what he saw when they met face to face. Her illness had aged her and she was six years older than he. But her genuine concern for him was growing, despite her efforts to conceal it under a light touch. "So," she wrote early in May, after receiving a letter from him saying that he had been suffering from a migraine headache,

> . . . when wise people happen to be ill, they sit up till six in the morning and get up again at nine?

> Do tell me how Lurias can ever be made out of such imprudences.[6]

Finally, on May 16, she capitulated to his repeated entreaties and her own wishes. "Come then. There will be truth and simplicity for you, in any case; and a friend." Browning's reply came swiftly the following day:

> I thank you for the leave you give me and for the infinite kindness of the way of giving it. I will call at 2 on Tuesday. . . .

On Tuesday the twentieth of May, 1845, Browning climbed the stairs of 50 Wimpole Street and entered Elizabeth's room. He arrived at three, which she had told him would be more convenient than two, and stayed until four-thirty. He came, as he later admitted, with a presentiment that he would fall in love, and he did so, immediately and completely. As for Elizabeth, this tall, strikingly handsome man, with his vitality and exultant joy in living, both excited and frightened her. The next morning she remarked to her father that she was actually "quite haunted by Mr. Browning," that it was almost a "persecution." [7] Mr. Barrett, assuming that Browning's visit, though unusual, was simply the compliment paid by a lesser poet to a greater, said reprovingly that she should not speak so of her friends. He did not take Browning seriously, and presumed that his daughter put as little importance on the occasion as he did himself. Mr. Barrett's oblivion to the romance progressing under his very nose was monumental; upon being told that Mr. Browning had called, a few weeks before his daughter left his house forever, he scoffed, "Yes, the man of the pomegranets!" [8]

Browning wrote to Elizabeth on the evening of that first visit, saying he hoped that he had not tired her by staying too long or talking too loudly. "I am proud and happy in your friendship, now and ever," he concluded, and asked if he might call again. Elizabeth answered immediately, saying that he might indeed come the following Tuesday, "and again, when you can and like together," and signed it, "Your friend, E. B."

Browning's reaction at receiving such an answer can be deduced from Elizabeth's letter written two days later, on May 24. Evidently ardor and impatience overcame his judgment, and he had written a letter in which he had said things which, to quote Elizabeth,

> . . . you will not say over again, nor unsay, but *forget at once,* and *forever, having said it all;* and which will die out between *you and me alone,* like a misprint between you and the printer. And this you will do *for my sake,* who am your friend (and you have none truer)—and this I ask because it is a condition necessary. . . .

She also said emphatically that if he ever said it again, or even referred to the episode, she would not receive him. She asked gently that he not be displeased with her; *"no, that* would be hail and lightning together." Browning replied at once, asking that she return the "misprint" to him if she had not already destroyed it. Significantly, she had not.

The offending letter was burned, and, for the time being, Browning accepted her disposition of him as a friend. Throughout the spring and summer he visited her almost every week, and they exchanged letters as often or oftener. Browning told her about his new book of poems, *Bells and Pomegranates VII: Dramatic Romances and Lyrics,* to be published that autumn. Elizabeth read both the manuscript and the proofs, commenting and usually praising. He wrote of his visits to Thomas Carlyle; she wrote of her letters from James Russell Lowell and Edgar Allan Poe. On July 8, she told him that she had actually gone for a walk with one of her sisters as far as Devonshire Gate, and Browning replied that he was delighted, but to be sure not to attempt too much too soon. Gradually her confidence in him grew, for he kept his promise and did not speak of love, though the ardor of his letters certainly communicated it to her in every line. Late in August she had come to trust him sufficiently to tell him about "Bro's" death, saying, "I have never said so much to a living being —I never *could* write or speak a word of it." [9] Browning replied by the evening post:

> I am *most* grateful, *most* grateful, dearest friend, for this admission to participate in any degree in these feelings . . . May God bless you,—in what is past and to come! I pray that from my heart, being yours.[10]

The situation might have continued unaltered, had not Mr. Barrett precipitated a family crisis. Elizabeth's health had improved so much that her doctor advised a winter in Italy. Her brothers and sisters encouraged the project, and so did Robert Browning. Then she broached the matter to her father. To her shocked bewilderment, he told her that she might do as she pleased, but that he would not permit any member of the family to accompany her. Since she could not travel alone, the entire project had to be abandoned. In vain Browning urged her to consider her duty to herself; but, though her obsessive devotion to her father had received a shattering blow, she would not risk angering him by leaving England. His wrath would fall on her brothers and sisters, and that, she felt, would be unfair. The episode did force her to see Browning in a new light, however, and evidently gave him courage to reopen the forbidden subject, for, on September 27, she wrote,

> You have touched me more profoundly than I thought even *you* could have touched me—my heart was full when you came here today. Henceforth I am yours for everything but to do you harm. . . .

And Browning answered, "My life is bound up with yours, my own, first and last love."

From that time on, the word "friend" was not mentioned between them. Browning was now permitted to call her "Ba," the pet name the family had given her when she was a child. He called on her as often as possible, but he frequently had to cut his visits short, because Elizabeth's health was sufficiently improved for her to see more people, and unexpected callers appeared. Not one of them—not even her most faithful visitors, Kenyon and Miss Mitford—had the remotest suspicion that Robert Browning considered himself engaged to Elizabeth Barrett and was doing his utmost to persuade her to be formally engaged to him. Miss Mitford pointedly disapproved of him, because he seemingly had no visible means of support. Browning was indignant when Elizabeth told him of this aspersion; he had never really cared for money until now, he told her, but he would prove himself capable of earning a living for her sake. Elizabeth replied gently that her income would be sufficient for them both, in Italy. They agreed that Kenyon must be told nothing, lest he feel impelled from a sense of honor and propriety to tell Mr. Barrett the truth. Mr. Barrett, for his part, continued supremely oblivious, even to the letters which came and went as often as three times a day.

The letters gave voice to Browning's confident joy, and Elizabeth's bewildered disbelief at first—"Could it be that heart and life were devastated to make room for you?—if so, it was well done—dearest!" [11]—followed by an equally ardent expression of joy: "You have come to me as a dream comes, as the best dreams come." [12] In December she sent him a ring and a lock of her hair, which he acknowledged, "I will live and die with your beautiful ring, your beloved hair—comforting me, blessing me." [13] Meanwhile, *Bells and Pomegranates VII* had appeared. "Now if people do not cry out about these poems, what are we to think of the world?" [14] Elizabeth demanded. But *Dramatic Romances and Lyrics* fell on almost deaf ears, despite the presence in the volume of such poems as "The Bishop Orders His Tomb," "Pictor Ignotus," "The Lost Leader," "Home Thoughts from Abroad," and part of "Saul." There was one little poem, called simply, "Song":

> Nay, but you who do not love her,
>   Is she not pure gold, my mistress?
> Holds earth aught—speak truth—above her?
>   Aught like this tress, see, and this tress,
> And this last fairest tress of all,
> So fair, see, ere I let it fall?

This poem, written for Elizabeth, certainly revealed to all who cared to read it, that Robert Browning was in the throes of an emotion hitherto unknown in his work, but since no one knew about his romance, the inspiration was not recognized.

By January, 1846, he was urgently importuning her to set a date for their marriage. He abhorred keeping secret what he longed to shout from the housetops. He wanted to speak to her father in the approved manner, and come to Wimpole Street openly as an accepted fiancé. Elizabeth, though her love had emboldened her considerably, was terrified.

> . . . the very approach to the subject is shut up by dangers, and . . . from the very moment of a suspicion entering *one* mind, we would never be able to meet again in this room . . . letters of yours, addressed to me here, would infallibly be stopped and destroyed, if not opened. Therefore it is advisable to hurry on nothing. . . .[15]

A week later, she wrote somberly,

> For *him* . . . he would rather see me dead at his foot than yield the point: and he will say so, and mean it, and persist in the meaning.[16]

Browning, faced with such monumental resistance, could only agree. He sent her the proofs of the final volume of *Bells and Pomegranates*, two plays not written for the stage: *Luria*, and *A Soul's Tragedy*. Both she praised in the highest terms. In spring, she began to go out for short walks and carriage drives. As the weather grew warmer, she paid calls and even visited Westminster Abbey. Browning rejoiced at her increasing strength, but he also realized that her greater involvment with the world beyond 50 Wimpole Street would put a correspondingly greater strain on the secrecy she had imposed. She had schooled herself to be on guard with her family (though by this time both Henrietta and Arabel were fully aware that their sister was in love), and with the few visitors she admitted. But one could never tell when a chance remark about "Mr. Browning" in a London drawing room might lead her to betray herself. As for Browning, he was never a good liar, and questions were beginning to be asked of him. He had already told his parents, who wholeheartedly approved. "Oh, dearest, let us marry and end all this!" he wrote on April 10, 1846, three days before the final issue of *Bells and Pomegranates* was published. He was so immersed in his attempts to persuade Elizabeth to come to a decision that the critical indifference to his latest work passed by him, almost unnoticed.

Elizabeth, however, still hesitated. Her father, she knew, had an almost pathological hatred of the idea of any of his children marrying, and she was terrified at the thought of being the first to offend him. Browning wrote constantly, two, three times a day. It never occurred to him to deliver an ultimatum, to demand that she choose between her father and himself. His love was great enough to permit him to continue in this same way for the rest of his life, if this was what Elizabeth wished; but he was far from convinced that she really did wish it. At the end of June he reminded her that they must make plans if they were to marry and go to Italy that year, for her health was still too precarious to risk traveling after September. "So you decide, here as elsewhere—but *do* decide," [17] he wrote, almost frantically. But she would not be hurried. "Seriously . . . there is time for deciding, is there not?" she wrote on June 27, plunging him into profound discouragement.

Nevertheless, he continued to make plans, writing to her about the relative merits of La Cava over Pisa in winter, and whether it might be better to travel overland than by ship. These letters she answered promptly and interestedly all through July and August, though still refusing to set a date. Then, once again, Mr. Barrett, all unknowing, brought matters to a crisis. On the tenth of September, Elizabeth wrote that "an edict has gone out." Wimpole Street was to be vacated, so that the house might be cleaned and renovated, and the family was to go to Tunbridge Wells. "Now—what *can* be done?" she asked.

No plans could be made at Tunbridge Wells. Browning could not even visit there. "You must decide. I will do as you wish." Browning, faced with the decision, made it unequivocally: "We must be *married directly* and go to Italy. I will go for the license today, and we can be married on Saturday." [18]

His resolute determination broke down her last resistance. On Saturday morning, September 12, 1846, accompanied only by Wilson, her maid, she met Browning at St. Marylebone Church. On the way she had nearly fainted, but a nearby chemist provided some *sal volatile,* so she was able to continue. Browning and his cousin James Silverthorne were waiting for her. "There was no elopement in the case, but simply a private marriage," [19] she wrote to her sisters from Italy, and the marriage was duly announced in the *Times* on September 21.

By preagreement, the couple parted immediately after the ceremony, to the astonishment of the officiating clergyman. As Elizabeth later explained, ". . . he [Robert] was reasonable enough, lest I should be unequal to the double exertion of the church and the railway on the same morning. . . ." [20] She returned to Wimpole Street, where, under cover of the family's preparation to go to Tunbridge Wells, she packed her belongings. "I did hate so to have to take off the ring," she wrote to her husband the next day. "You will have to take the trouble of putting it on one day." [21] Browning replied, "I exult in the irrevocability of this precious bestowal of yourself on—me—come what will my life has born flower and fruit—it is a glorious, successful, felicitous life, I thank God and you." [22] He also practically advised her not to carry much luggage. She could buy whatever she needed at Leghorn or Pisa. In his excitement, he misread the timetable for the Southampton boat train, and Elizabeth had to unsnarl the tangle.

Finally all was ready. On the evening of September 19,

Browning met Elizabeth, Wilson, and the cocker spaniel Flush—who could not possibly be left behind—at Vauxhall Station. At nine o'clock, they were safely aboard the Channel steamer for Le Havre. The passage was rough, and Browning, who was now for the first time in his life responsible not alone for the happiness, but actually for the life of another person, was nearly frantic with anxiety. When they reached Le Havre on the following morning, he insisted that they remain there the entire day so that Elizabeth might rest. Then, gently, tenderly overcoming his wife's inevitable reaction of depression at the thought of what her happiness must be costing her brothers and sisters by her "having given pain by a voluntary act," [23] he booked seats aboard the night diligence to Rouen.

They arrived there at one o'clock in the morning. Elizabeth, though exhausted, was eager to continue the journey. Browning debated the wisdom of it, but finally decided that the more distance they put between themselves and England, the better; so he carried Elizabeth into the Travelers' Room at the station to wait and get what rest she could. A few hours later, they were roaring through Normandy on the new express which would bring them to Paris the next morning. He saw with great anxiety that Elizabeth, despite her courage and high spirits, looked very frail, and was grateful that Wilson was with them. Upon being assured by his wife that she really was feeling better, and that she would be perfectly well once they reached Italy, his old confidence returned. Elizabeth was his, at last, and search the wide world over, where she was, there would be the glorious life he had envisioned for them both, and which was even now filled with more joy than he had hoped. He could hardly believe his own good fortune.

6

Immediately upon their arrival in Paris, after seeing that Elizabeth was comfortably settled at their hotel and ordering Wilson to put her to bed at once, Browning went round to the Hotel de Ville, where Elizabeth's devoted friend Mrs. Jameson was staying. Mrs. Jameson had not been told of the impending marriage, because they both knew that she would have heartily disapproved and moved heaven and earth to prevent it. She had more than once informed Elizabeth in no uncertain terms that she was not at all impressed with Robert Browning. Her objection, like Miss Mitford's, was his financial status, and Browning was ruefully aware that she was justified in her conclusions, having had to borrow a hundred pounds from his father to finance the journey. She was, however, too sensible and too good a friend not to amiably accept a *fait accompli*. She called on them that same evening and found Elizabeth looking, as she later wrote friends in England, "frightfully ill." Nevertheless, whatever practical objections she might have had soon vanished as she recognized Browning's attentive care and love for his wife, and Elizabeth's own obvious happiness. "He is a wise man . . . and *you* are a wise woman, let the world say as it pleases," [1] she told Elizabeth upon leaving. For the most sensible of reasons she immediately vetoed their plan to leave at once for Italy, insisted that they take a suite near her own at the Hotel de Ville, and literally commanded them to stay in Paris at least a week before continuing south.

For this summary management, Browning was grateful.

When Elizabeth indicated that it would be pleasant to have Mrs. Jameson travel with them, since she was going to Italy anyway, he did not demur. The idea of a third person on a honeymoon may seem incongruous in the twentieth century, but, in the Victorian era, it was quite customary for a bride to have a "female companion" travel with her; and Elizabeth's health made the presence of a lady possessed of strong mind and a good common sense, who knew all the necessities of feminine travel as he himself did not, seem reasonable and even desirable. Also, Browning knew that, sooner or later, Elizabeth would have letters from her family in answer to the notes she had left for them, which might distress her terribly. It would be well to have Mrs. Jameson, who now so wholeheartedly approved of them, on hand to reassure her.

He was correct in this surmise. When they arrived at Orléans on September 29, a packet of letters was waiting for his wife. He gave them to her, and watched anxiously, for she made no effort to open them—merely sat holding them, her trembling hands like ice. At last she asked him to leave her, while she read the letter from her father. When she called him, he found her stunned. He sat beside her for several hours, trying to console her, for the harshness of Mr. Barrett's letter was beyond belief. He had told his daughter that she had sold her soul for *"genius . . . mere genius,"* [2] and that henceforth he would consider her as dead. The letter from her brother George was quite as shocking; he said that she had sacrificed all delicacy and honor. Browning's fury at the male Barretts must have been intense, but he wisely refrained from criticism, for which Elizabeth was deeply grateful. Fortunately the letters from Henrietta and Arabel were all she could have wished, and a note of unequivocal approval from John Kenyon further mitigated a blow which, though anticipated, was most difficult to bear. Even Miss Mitford kindly wished them well. Elizabeth immediately answered all the letters, including the one from her father, for she was certain that he could not continue obdurate for too long, especially when she herself was so very happy, and knew herself so greatly loved. Browning hoped, for her sake, that she was right; privately he was none too sure, but concealed his doubts.

The journey provided further distractions. Browning took her to Bourges for a day, to visit the cathedral with its remarkable stained-glass windows. Next came a trip by diligence to Lyons, where they boarded the Rhone River steamer for Avignon. Much to Elizabeth's disappointment, it poured rain, so that they could not see the Alps for the mist. At Avignon, Browning toured the papal palace with Mrs. Jameson, while Elizabeth stayed at the hotel to rest, for the down-river trip had been tiring, especially since she had been emotionally exhausted before boarding the steamer. But by the time they reached Vaucluse, where Petrarch had lived, she was able to walk to the famous churning pool. Suddenly, to her husband's amazement, she gaily broke away and started to walk across the rocks alone. "Ba, are you losing your senses?" he called and ran after her, Flush barking at his heels. He caught up with her, laughing, midway, and they sat down on one of the boulders, while Mrs. Jameson, who had remained on shore, sketched them.

From Vaucluse they traveled to Marseilles, where they embarked for Leghorn. The steamer stopped at Genoa for a day and they went ashore. Browning took Elizabeth for a walk through the narrow streets and into one of the churches. He had visited many Italian churches in his own travels, and was eager to share their beauty with her. She was enthralled by the gold-encrusted marble altar and the frescoed angels on the ceiling. Then they returned to the steamer, and, after a stormy passage, reached Leghorn the next morning. A few hours later, on October 13, they reached their final destination, Pisa.

Browning's intention had been only to winter in Italy and to return to England in the spring. But when Mr. Barrett did not answer any of Elizabeth's letters, he decided that, though his father-in-law might relent, they had better not count on it. A hotel would serve temporarily, but if they must remain in Pisa longer, they would have to have a more permanent home. Also, the sooner Elizabeth became accustomed to the idea of actually living out of England, the better, and managing a home of their own would make the transition easier for her. So, after a few days, he leased an apartment in the Collegio Ferdinando, a stone's throw from the cathedral and the Leaning Tower. That the Collegio Ferdinando had been designed by Vasari, whose *Lives of the Painters* Browning had read avidly as a boy, was probably its major recommendation—that, and its reasonable rent. For though he had to depend upon Elizabeth's income, he did not intend to have it said that he was extravagant with his wife's money.

The winter passed quietly and uneventfully. Browning put aside his poetry and devoted himself to caring for his wife. Her health had improved so greatly, and her dependence on morphine had so much lessened that, as early as November, he could write to her sisters that if they could see her, "so changed as to be hardly recognizable, and with a fair prospect of life and enjoyment for many years to come," [3] even their father would surely agree that the marriage had been wise. His infinite concern for her is evident from the final paragraph in that letter:

> And now, may I ask you a favor? It is, that if anything should strike you with respect to Ba's

well-being . . . any suggestion that you may think of for her comfort—you will write of it to *me*—not to *her*, with her unselfish, generous disregard of what she fancies (most erroneously) to relate exclusively to herself—in all probability I should never hear of it—but for a hint, a word to *me* directly, I shall be very grateful.[4]

Elizabeth continued to grow stronger, and by spring both she and Browning had decided that Pisa was almost too quiet: Florence would suit them better, they thought, and Elizabeth was ready for Florence, now. So, in April, Robert packed their trunks and they boarded the diligence. In Florence they took lodgings for a time, but by August, 1847, they were settled in Casa Guidi, near Pitti Palace. This was to be their home for fifteen years.

The Browning marriage is generally presented as a continuation of the Browning romance, and, in a sense, they did remain, as they have been called, "immortal lovers." Certainly Browning made no secret of his adoration of his wife, and she quite literally worshipped him. It is true that they thoroughly enjoyed each other's company, to the extent that, even when Elizabeth was able to go about socially, they tended to keep to themselves. It was not that they especially sought to avoid the English colony at Florence, so much as that they really enjoyed each other and the stimulation of their own work more. Naturally all doors were open to them, starting with Mrs. Frances Trollope's. Mrs. Trollope, mother of the novelist Anthony Trollope, had an enormous palazzo and entertained lavishly; Browning, however, found her rather boisterous and vulgar and found excellent reasons for not accepting her invitations. He did enjoy the company of Hiram Powers, the American sculptor, and of George William Curtis, who had been a member of Bronson Alcott's Brooke Farm community, and could talk most entertainingly about Hawthorne and Emerson. But there was so much to see in Florence—the art galleries, the palaces and bridges, the piazzas and coloñ̃ades. Why spend time sipping tea in stuffy drawing rooms, when all about them was the Renaissance incarnate? In this Elizabeth agreed. The teas and the people were charming, but they left little strength or time for doing other things quite as important.

Not only the Renaissance surrounded them, but the new Italy as well. The Brownings arrived in Florence just as the Risorgimento—the Italian struggle to gain freedom from Austria—was beginning. The dream of a free united Italy had been born in the days of Bonaparte, had been kept alive by a secret society called the Carbonari, and finally had become the battle of Giuseppe Mazzini and his organization called Young Italy. Mazzini had been driven into exile in the thirties, and had lived for many years in London. Since Carlyle had befriended him, it is reasonable to suppose that Browning may have met him at Carlyle's home. Through agents in England and Switzerland, Mazzini carried on his intrigues against Austria, most of them unsuccessful, until May, 1846, when a new pope with more liberal ideas than those of his predecessors was elected, and opened the way to fulfilment of the dream.

At that time, Italy was split into a number of small principalities, whose rulers governed more or less according to decrees issued from Vienna. The new pope, Pius IX—"Pio Nonno"—was not only spiritual head of the Roman Catholic Church, he was also ruler of the Papal States, where most repressive measures had been taken against would-be revolutionaries. Pio Nonno lifted some of these restrictions, lightened the strangling censorship, and proclaimed a general amnesty to all political exiles, thus permitting Mazzini and his friends to return to Italy. All Europe cheered the new pope's liberality, none more enthusiastically than Robert Browning. Hearing that England might send an ambassador to the Papal States, he had written enthusiastically to Richard Monckton-Milnes (an old friend who was combining the profession of poet with a highly successful career in Parliament) that "he would be glad and proud to be secretary to such an embassy, and would work like a horse for it." [5] His offer, however, was not accepted.

When Austria, disturbed at the rumors of insurrection, sent a military force to occupy Farrara, the pope's protest at this aggression caused another thunderous wave of approval across Italy, and there were immediate uprisings in Genoa, Milan, and Naples, so that by the time the Brownings reached Florence in April, 1847, the revolution had already arrived. Leopold II, grand duke of Tuscany, a kindly despot whom his people called their *Gran Chinco,* "great donkey," seeing the way the wind blew, lifted the censorship of the press. In September he granted the people the right to establish a civic guard, the first time Florentines had been permitted to bear arms in half a century. On the day of their first wedding anniversary, Browning watched at the window of Casa Guidi while a huge demonstration passed them on the way to Pitti Palace to cheer the grand duke. Elizabeth was thrilled to tears at the sight. Two weeks later, Leopold granted the city a constitution, and Florence went mad. The grand duke went to the opera incognito, but he was recognized and carried home after the performance on the shoulders of his cheering subjects. On Sundays thereafter the new guard paraded in their uniforms, much to Elizabeth's delight, which she expressed in long letters to her sisters, and in *Casa Guidi Windows,* the new poem on which she was working. Browning, however, had reservations. "Surely after all this, they would *use* those muskets," [6] he thought worriedly, for he knew better than his wife what the use of the muskets would mean.

But neither he nor anyone else anticipated the holocaust that the year 1848 brought not only to Italy, but to all Europe. In February, word came that Louis Philippe, king of France, had been deposed. Within days, Naples and Sicily rose against their King Ferdinand, demanding and obtaining a constitution. Ferdinand of Naples was a puppet of Austria, but, realizing that his subjects were ready to depose him if he did not accede to their demands, declared war on Austria and sent his army to meet the enemy force stationed at Pavia. The rebellion spread to Milan, where, after five desperate days in March, the Austrian army was actually driven beyond the frontier of Lombardy. On March 12, Venice declared itself a republic. On March 13, Pio Nonno gave way to the demands of the revolutionaries, and granted a constitution to Rome. From Florence, Browning wrote to Henrietta and Arabel Barrett,

> Don't feel the least alarm at the rumors of wars
> that fill the world—I mean alarm on her account
> —I will not be caught sleeping, I promise . . . The
> cowardly English are leaving the place—infinitely to
> the satisfaction of the less mouse-hearted who stay,
> not being frightened at their own shadows; should
> our city be entered,—we can reach Leghorn in a few
> hours and find a hundred merchant vessels, *plus*
> the squadron from Malta, which will arrive at the
> first warning of hostilities, but nothing of the kind
> will be needed, in all probability. All the excitement
> and busy sense of life does Ba good. . . .[7]

Upper left. Casa Guidi, Florence. Browning's rooms were on the second floor, just above the tablet, which was dedicated to Mrs. Browning's memory by the Florentines. **Upper right.** 19 Warwick Crescent, Paddington, London. Browning's residence from 1861 to 1887. **Lower left.** 29 De Vere Gardens, Kensington. Browning's last home in London. He occupied it from 1887 to 1889. **Lower right.** The Palazzo Rezzonico, Venice, where Browning died, December 12, 1889. *The Prints Division, The New York Public Library.*

New address. 19. Warwick Crescent,
Upper Westbourne Terrace.
Apr. 28. '62.

Dearest Friends,

Only time for a word, but that a
good one. I have just seen Pompiani (who
is here in some conservative capacity - you
remember his going to the studio with Mad.
de Guerine?) & he assures me that Both
Statues are well placed, in good light,
"each opposite the other" in a good arrange-
ment": - & this moment, see what I said
in the "Times" - Apr. 28.

In the Roman Court, as might be expected, are
some noble groups of statuary & mosaics. In 1851 the
"Greek Slave" the work of an American artist carried
off all the honors of sculpture, and again on this
occasion, we think the laurels will be awarded
to another American student, Mr Storey, who has

Letter from Browning to William Wetmore Story, the American
sculptor and poet. Dated April 28, 1862, it was sent from 19 Warwick Crescent.
From the author's collection.

Then events took an unexpected turn. On April 29, Pio Nonno published an Allocution, censuring the revolutionaries and proclaiming that he would not sanction war against Catholic Austria. The pressures on him to "maintain peace" made any other course impossible; nevertheless, he lost the support of his many admirers, and by the end of the year he, too, was a fugitive. Meanwhile, Austria, gaining strength from his pronouncement, sent reinforcements, and the Italian armies were soundly beaten at Custozza in July. On the Swiss border, a rag-and-bobtail army in red shirts under the command of Giuseppi Garibaldi fought a diversionary action, but they were compelled to withdraw and disperse. An armistice was declared and the war with Austria was over. "Dante's soul has died out of this land," [8] Elizabeth wrote to her friend Miss Mitford, bemoaning the pope's Allocution and the seeming cowardice of the Italians, who refused to stand fast when everything looked to be in their favor. She approved the French revolution highly; their king, Louis Philippe, was now living in England, an exile, and the French deputies had elected Louis Napoleon, Bonaparte's nephew, president of the Republic. Browning, however, did not agree with his wife's estimate of Louis Napoleon; he thought the man a shrewd opportunist who concealed his lust for power under a veil of patriotism and humanitarianism. There were many spirited arguments in Casa Guidi.

Browning, however, had greater concerns than the fate of Italy or of the French Republic. Elizabeth was expecting a child and had already suffered two miscarriages. Though the military actions of the revolution had been terminated by the armistice, the Risorgimento itself had merely gone underground, and outbreaks of violence were frequent. In November, 1848, Browning wrote to his sisters-in-law, "Don't fear whatever you may read or hear, —I will be very watchful, depend on it, and anticipate the least real danger. . . ." [9] The winter months passed in anxious waiting, and his joy and relief were indescribable when Robert Wiedemann Barrett Browning was born on March 9, 1849.

> This is being written on the 9th of March at
> 4 o'clock in the morning to tell you that thro' God's
> infinite goodness our blessed Ba gave birth to a fine,
> strong boy at quarter past two: and is doing
> admirably.[10]

the proud father wrote Henrietta and Arabel. Strangely enough, his son arrived in the midst of a tumult equal to that surrounding his own birth, thirty-seven years before in Camberwell. On March 12, the people of Florence, angered by the truce with Austria and the additional restrictions it put on them, rose in revolt and drove out the grand duke. Browning watched from his window while a jubilant crowd planted a tree of liberty, to the booming of cannon and ringing of bells. For a few brief days there was a republic; then, a hastily assembled Italian army, Garibaldi's red shirts among them, was decisively defeated at Novara on March 23. The grand duke returned to Florence under Austrian escort; there was fighting and bloodshed in the streets. The tree of liberty was uprooted and the revolution was over.

Browning's concern for his wife and infant son was enormous, and, though he had remained ever watchful, he breathed a great sigh of relief when the danger was past. His letters written during this period which have survived say nothing about the political upheaval in Florence; they are devoted to ecstatic descriptions of his son.

> He is the sweetest little creature you can imagine,
> so strong and lively—and good, except when they

> plague him with dressings and washings in which
> Flush deeply sympathizes with him . . . And, do you
> know, he follows lights and noises with his great
> eyes, and even hands—and when I make a chirrup
> to him with my lips, fairly takes hold of my nose! [11]

Now that the country had become fairly calm, they began to plan for a journey to England. Browning was eager for his parents to see their first grandchild; Elizabeth was certain that her father must certainly succumb to the baby's charm, and thus a reconciliation could be effected. But this happy prospect had to be abandoned, when Browning received a letter from his father, long delayed by the war, saying that his mother had died a few days after his son's birth.

Browning had always been very close to his mother, and the news of her death plunged him into such a depth of grief that he could neither eat nor sleep properly for weeks. He could not bear the thought of returning to England, now that she was no longer there. Elizabeth worried about him constantly, and finally she decided that he must have a change of scene. Browning reluctantly agreed, and early in the summer the entire household moved to a villa in Bagni di Lucca in the mountains. For the first few days his depression seemed to increase, if anything, but gradually his spirits began to revive, especially since his wife and baby were so well. Elizabeth roamed the hills with him, and the entire family often picnicked beside the waterfall, an ideal situation for relaxation and peace of mind. It was at Villa Bagni di Lucca that Elizabeth gave him, one morning after breakfast, the collection of sonnets which she had begun during their courtship, later to be known as *Sonnets from the Portuguese*. He read them at one sitting, deeply moved, and declared that they were the finest sonnets in any language except Shakespeare's. He was intensely proud of his wife, and grateful to her as well. Her open and unselfconscious avowal of love in the sonnets in no small measure healed his grief over his mother's death. And—even more important—they seemed to spark his own creative spirit. By the time their holiday ended, he was again working at his own poetry, and when they returned to Florence in October, he was well launched into a major work, *Christmas Eve and Easter Day*.

Robert Browning was a deeply religious man. Apart from his brief excursion into atheism under the influence of Shelley's poetry, he had never seriously doubted the existence of God, and he had always found great strength and comfort in the evangelical beliefs which his mother had taught him. But evangelical chapels were usually plain, almost bleak, and his poetic sensitivity responded to the beauty of the Roman Catholic churches and the formality of their liturgy. In addition, yet apart from these, his intellect was stimulated by the new scientific approach to the Bible. It is most unlikely that he would not have read George Eliot's translation of Strauss's *Das Leben Jesu,* published in 1846, which took the rationalist position that Jesus was the greatest and best of men, but still only a man. Neither of these two influences had affected him sufficiently to make him consider changing his expression of faith. But his mother's death forced him to face the fact that, subconsciously, he had been questioning and meditating for quite some time; he set himself the task of writing a poem with the spiritual hope of finding his own answer to two questions: "What do I truly believe about God?" and, "On what is my faith grounded?" He had Elizabeth's encouragement in the project; she had long urged him to write something wherein he would speak to the world in his own voice, and express his own philosophy and belief.

He did not go quite that far, but at least he drew on his own thought and experience sufficiently to make *Christmas Eve and Easter Day* a more personal poem than he usually wrote, and one of the most remarkable religio-philosophical poems in the language. His description of the nineteenth-century evangelical chapel and its congregation, "The hot smell and the human noises," is devastating, almost satiric in its accuracy, and it is not surprising to hear the narrator say, "I very soon had enough of it." He leaves the chapel to walk under the stars and contemplates how God's great power

> Was to create man and then leave him
> Able, his own word saith to grieve him,
> But able to glorify him too,
> As a mere machine could never do. . . .

His thoughts turn to death—how death can come

> . . . and choose about me,
> And my dearest ones depart without me.

Then, suddenly, the sky is ablaze with light, and a perfect lunar rainbow appears. Trembling he watches—then,

> All at once I looked up with terror.
> He was there.

Many years later, Robert Browning, upon being prodded, denied emphatically that he was the "I" of the poem. But he did admit to having seen the lunar rainbow. That his mother's death had been a tremendous crisis in his life is obvious, and that the crisis had led to some sort of mystical experience, leading him to a direct perception of the power of Eternal Love as the "sole good of life" is possible and understandable. But, characteristically, for Browning was a man of action, the "I" of *Christmas Eve and Easter Day* is not permitted to remain in undisturbed contemplation. Clinging to the hem of God's floating garment, he is carried aloft, and has a vision of Christmas Eve Midnight Mass at St. Peter's in Rome.

> For see, for see, the rapturous moment
> Approaches. . . .
> Earth breaks up, time drops away,
> In flows heaven with its new day
> Of endless life, when He who trod,
> Very man and very God,
> This earth in weakness, shame and pain,
> Dying the death whose signs remain
> Up yonder on the accursed tree,—
> Shall come again, no more to be
> Of captivity the thrall,
> But the one God, All in all,
> King of kings, Lord of lords,
> As His servant John received the words,
> "I died, and live forevermore!"

He is deeply moved at the sight and cries swiftly,

> I *see* the error; but above
> The scope of error, *see the love*. [Italics mine.—R. S.]

Rome to the speaker (as to Robert Browning), had always been the symbol of error, hypocrisy, and distortion of truth, but he knows now that he must look beyond the surface; even though he cannot enter into the mass, he can understand the love which prompts this—to him—alien way.

This new perception makes possible his tolerance of the learned professor in the second vision, who is delivering a lecture on the "historic Jesus," stripping religion of all elements of the miraculous, enjoining his audience to follow the teachings of Christ, but to remember that He was only a man. The narrator listens quietly, acknowledges the professor's probable sincerity of belief, but asks the crucial question:

> Thus much of Christ does he reject?
> And what retain? His intellect?
> What is it I must reverence duly?
> Pure intellect for worship, truly,
> Which tells me simply what was told
> (If mere morality, bereft
> Of the God in Christ, be all that's left)
> Elsewhere by voices manifold;
> With this advantage, that the stater
> Made nowise the important stumble
> Of adding, he, the sage and humble,
> Was also one with the Creator.

The end of *Christmas Eve* finds him back in the evangelical chapel, having chosen it as the place,

> Where earthly aids being cast behind,
> His All in All appears serene
> With the thinnest human veil between. . . .

He has acquired the grace and humility to look beyond the drab surroundings, the commonplace people, and even the platitudinous sermon, to the God Whom he knows he must worship.

Having justified his expression of faith, Browning then turned to the more thorny problem of faith itself. The *Easter Day* section of the poem is cast in the form of a dialogue between two Christians. One finds the Christian belief easy to accept, but he does not have much depth. The other begins by saying, "How very hard it is to be a

Christian!" and searches desperately for tangible proof that God exists, so that he may have some intellectual basis for his act of faith.

> At first you say, "The whole, or chief
> Of difficulties, is belief.
> Could I believe once thoroughly,
> The rest were simple. What? Am I
> An idiot, do you think,—a beast?"

For a man of intellect, blind faith simply will not do. This was Browning's own dilemma, and the dilemma of many nineteenth-century intellectuals. It was the subject of discussions, lectures and magazine articles. Battered by the new Biblical scholarship on the one hand, and the new scientific theories which were to culminate in Darwin's *Origin of Species* in 1859, on the other, the simple act of belief seemed a renunciation of the knowledge they were supposed to advance and the truth they were supposed to uphold.

Easter Day also has its projected vision, of the Last Judgment. In one magnificent passage, reminiscent of the Book of Revelation, the intellectual man sees himself before the throne of God, and realizes that, instead of seeking to love and know God through the world, he has chosen to love the world itself, "So beautiful, so near." He hears the ominous words,

> . . . "Life is done,
> Time ends, Eternity's begun,
> And thou art judged forevermore."

He is not one who could find God in nature, for the beauty of nature arrests his interest and pleasure too easily to look beyond it. Desperately he calls upon Art to lead him to belief, for the artist in the act of creation stands

very near to the Creator Himself. But the mystical voice
tells him that this will not be the way.

> "The one form with its single act,
> Which sculptors labored to abstract,
> The one face, painters tried to draw,
> With its one look, from throngs they saw,
> And that perfection in their soul,
> These only hinted at? . . ."

The artist's vision can only indicate the perfection of creation itself.

Frantic, now, the speaker says that he will follow the
way of intellect.

> "Let me, since I can fly no more,
> At least spin dervish-like about
> (Till giddy rapture almost doubt
> I fly) through circling sciences,
> Philosophies and histories!
> Should the whirl slacken there, then verse,
> Fining to music, shall asperse
> Fresh and fresh fire-dew, till I strain
> Intoxicate, half-break my chain!"

But what of those intangibles that will not yield to ab-
stract reasoning or to scientific investigation? He realizes
in a sudden flash that his intellect, too, is earthbound,
when it has made no room for the spiritual, those "intui-
tions, grasps of guess," beyond the probing of mortal mind.
At last he cries, "I let the world go, and take love!" For
the first time, his judge seems to approve his choice but
the end is not yet. Earthly love is only the echo of God's
love, and true man cannot truly experience whole love if
he casts aside "him who made the whole." That Love is
the beginning of faith. The speaker, cowering, answers
humbly,

"Thou, love of God! Or let me die" . . .
Then did the form expand, expand—
I knew him through the dread disguise
As the whole God within his eyes
Embraced me.

Christmas Eve and Easter Day is a very much neglected poem in contemporary criticism. It was equally neglected by the readers of 1850, the year of its publication, who, for the most part, found it rather dry and ascetic in tone, but did not sense why. The evangelicals resented the graphic description of the chapel; the Roman Catholics and High Anglicans admired the descriptions of the Midnight Mass and the Last Judgment, but resented the poet's conclusion that they were in error. The deeper meanings eluded most readers and critics alike.

The poem is, however, crucial to an understanding of Robert Browning's development as a man and a poet. The discipline of thinking through his own religious beliefs clarified and stabilized his convictions. The poem also reveals that he did not arrive at his optimism, for which he has been censured, without considerable struggle. His was not the easy optimism based on a theory of man's inevitable progress, but rather on a firm act of faith that, since God was in His heaven, all would be right with the world, despite appearances to the contrary. From 1850 on, there is hardly one of his poems which does not in some way reflect his own hard-won faith in that Love as the informing, sustaining power of the universe—a Love that infuses grief, sorrow, sin, even death itself, and can transmute the most sordid circumstance into glorious opportunity for the man who believes to progress to the state of perfection for which he was created.

7

The winter of 1849-50 had been both busy and productive. Robert Browning had finished *Christmas Eve and Easter Day,* and Elizabeth Barrett Browning had revised all her poems and added a number of new ones, including the *Sonnets from the Portuguese,* for publication in a new collected edition. But work had not prevented their enjoying numerous visitors. Mornings were given to writing; afternoons to receiving friends and acquaintances, or to being entertained themselves. Florence had been very gay that winter. Among these several visitors had come Margaret Fuller, one of the first members of the New England transcendentalist group, and first editor of the *Dial.* She had married an Italian nobleman the Marchese Ossoli, and had nursed the wounded during the abortive revolution in Rome. She became a close friend of the Brownings, despite her enthusiasm for socialism in which Browning did not concur. Nevertheless, the Marchesa was one of his staunchest admirers. "Mr. Browning enriches every hour I spend with him, and is a most cordial, true, and noble man," she wrote in her *Memoirs.* Both of the Brownings were shocked and grieved to learn of her death in a shipwreck off Fire Island, New York, in the summer of 1850, a disaster in which her husband and infant son also perished.

An even happier friendship was that of Miss Isabella Blagden, "Isa," a "bright, delicate, electric woman," as Browning described her, who lived in a villa outside Florence and augmented her small income by writing novels. Isa was an intelligent, witty woman, who offered intellectual stimulation to both poets when they needed it, and light conversation and gossip when they needed diversion. She and Elizabeth shared a sympathetic bond in their mutual admiration of Louis Napoleon, but Browning was no more enthusiastic about him than about socialism. Louis Napoleon had assisted Pio Nonno in regaining control of the Papal States after his ignominious flight, and was now issuing pompous censures from Paris about the pope's mismanagement of his little kingdom, a course which Browning found fundamentally inconsistent. Nor did he care for the French president's highhandedness in raising his own salary by increasing taxes, and then spending the money on feasts to insure the loyalty of his army. It seemed to him that the man's professed liberal sentiments were giving way to expediency, a view which he was to uphold later in his satiric poem, *Prince Hohenstiel-Schwangau, Saviour of Society*.

Money was a constant problem that winter, for prices were high in the aftermath of revolution. Browning had hoped to take his family to England during the summer, but the sales of *Christmas Eve and Easter Day* were not sufficient to justify such expense. Then, at the end of July, 1850, Elizabeth suffered her last and most serious miscarriage. Browning, writing desperately to John Kenyon, said that she had lost over a hundred ounces of blood in twenty-four hours; this was in a day when blood-transfusion was unknown and the hot Florentine summer further sapped her energy. She was very slow in regaining her strength. Their little boy, too, had suffered greatly from the heat. Not until September were they both well enough to travel for a few weeks' stay in the hills above Siena until the chilly autumn winds brought them back to Florence. To Browning's infinite relief and gratitude, his wife seemed much better, indeed well enough to work steadily through the fall and winter at her new volume, *Casa Guidi Windows*. The high point of that winter was a visit in December from Goethe's grandson, who made the trip to Florence especially to see Robert Browning and to discuss *Paracelsus* with him.

Another favorite visitor during the early part of 1851 was Charles Eliot Norton, soon to be first Professor of Fine Arts at Harvard. He came often to Casa Guidi to discuss books and paintings, and he and Browning became close friends. "He is quite unconscious and never even in the slightest way claims any regard for himself as a poet, or shows that he expects you to remember that he is one," Norton wrote to an American friend. "Indeed, one of the most charming characteristics of both himself and his wife is their self-forgetfulness." [1]

By spring Elizabeth was strong enough so that the long-anticipated visit to England could become a reality. The Browning finances were still shaky, but tenants were found for Casa Guidi, which helped. Their son was now two years old, and no longer needed a special nurse; Wilson could manage him nicely, though Robert Wiedemann Barrett Browning was active enough to keep an entire household occupied. He had long since started to walk and to chatter, and he had given himself a name—Pen, short for "Penini," which was his interpretation of Wiedemann, the name his parents had planned to call him. Pen thus early demonstrated that independence which was to be his chief characteristic as he grew older. He was a beautiful child, with long blond hair which Elizabeth refused to cut, and his dresses—all little boys wore dresses in 1851—were of velvet since the weather was still cool, which made him quite a striking figure among the children of the neighborhood. Browning worried about the dresses; he had repeatedly suggested that Elizabeth put the child in trousers, or at least cut his hair, but she refused to do so. It was as though she regretted the thought of having Pen grow up, so her husband did not insist.

Early in May, 1851, accompanied by Wilson and, naturally, Flush, the Brownings left Florence for a month's stay in Venice and might have remained longer, had Browning not been taken ill. "So exquisite—and so bilious," [2] was Elizabeth's wry comment on the canal city in her letter to Miss Mitford. Milan was the next stop; then they crossed into Switzerland via the St. Gotthard Pass and arrived in Lucerne with just ten francs between them. Fortunately some money, though not the amount they had hoped, had been sent there for them from England, and they decided to continue as inexpensively as possible by rail and diligence to Paris. Here they unexpectedly met Alfred Tennyson, the recently appointed poet laureate, and his wife, who were on their way to Italy. The Brownings saw a great deal of them during their short stay, and Tennyson generously offered his house at Twickenham for their visit to England. But Twickenham was too far from Wimpole Street, and, when the Brownings reached London late in July, they leased a small apartment in Devonshire Place.

The real purpose of the trip to England was to make an attempt at reconciliation with Mr. Barrett. Elizabeth had sent letter after letter to her father, but had received no reply. Her brothers, with the exception of George, who had relented, had been equally silent, an attitude which she thought most unfair, for they had all remained on friendly terms with Henrietta who had recently defied her father and married a distant cousin, Captain Surtees Cook. Henrietta, Arabel, and George were the only Barretts who called on the Brownings, or even acknowledged their existence. Finally Robert Browning wrote a firm letter to Mr.

Barrett, enclosing one from Elizabeth in which she begged that he at least see his grandson. In reply they received a violent, angry note, with two packets of Elizabeth's letters, their seals unbroken. Browning, who had electrified passers-by by kissing the threshold of St. Marylebone Church where he had been married, was furious, but nothing could be done. His own father and sister, however, welcomed Elizabeth and Pen with open arms, and friends saw that the visiting poets were royally entertained. Carlyle, John Forster, and Mrs. Jameson came to call; John Kenyon gave a dinner party in their honor, and within a few days' time at other parties they met the American journalist and poet Bayard Taylor, and Fanny Kemble, niece of the great Sarah Siddons, who was making a considerable reputation as an actress herself. By the time the September fog began to settle over London, Elizabeth's spirits were greatly restored. Browning had decided that a winter in Paris might provide a further distraction for her. Their traveling companion on the trip was Thomas Carlyle, who kept Elizabeth amused by his vigorous, picturesque observations of the rough Channel crossing, and, later, of French railways generally. Browning was left to cope with the luggage—a situation which he found highly entertaining. A poet, shepherding a philosopher!

They arrived in Paris to find the city torn apart by the latest decrees of Louis Napoleon. According to law, the president could not serve two terms successively, but Louis Napoleon had conveniently discovered that the particular law had never been properly ratified. Also, many of the people had grown weary of "Citizen Rule" and longed for the glorious days of Napoleon Bonaparte. In late November, Louis Napoleon appealed to the people to support him, and on December 2, he entered Paris with his army behind him. The republicans set up barricades in the streets, and Louis Napoleon retaliated with guns. On December 4, the Brownings heard the cannonading of the "Massacre of the Boulevards," in which over twelve hundred civilians died. A few days later, Bonaparte's nephew was elected to a ten-year term as president by acclamation, but many perceptive observers, Robert Browning among them, were aware that this was only a preliminary step towards the title he really wanted—that of emperor.

Browning settled down to a winter of work in the apartment they had rented on the Champs Élysées. He planned, he announced, to write a poem a day. He was also writing an introduction to a volume of Shelley's letters which had recently been discovered. Still there was time to visit the Louvre, to attend the Opéra, to see a performance of Dumas' new play *La Dame aux camélias,* and to attend a reception in honor of the poet Alfred de Musset. James T. Fields, the Boston publisher, called to see about bringing out an American edition of Elizabeth's poems. They were also received by the novelist whom Elizabeth admired above all others, George Sand, but they found her cigars and trousers and brusque manner rather disconcerting. Browning's father and sister crossed the Channel to visit them. Elizabeth continued well, and was busily working on *Aurora Leigh,* her novel in verse. Pen, though delicate and highly strung, was vociferous as ever, now freely mixing French with his Italian and English, and greatly enjoying the Punch-and-Judy shows he saw in his afternoon walks on the Champs Élysées. Paris seemed to be doing them all good.

Nevertheless, there is evidence that Browning's contentment was often marred by an inner restlessness. Elizabeth wrote to one of her sisters that he would have been perfectly happy to remain in England, had it been possible. His few months' visit had revived many loved memories, and his family and closest friends lived there. Though he loved Italy, his heart was in the gardens of Camberwell, too. "Oh, to be in England now that April's there," he had written nostalgically. He loved London. It would be only natural for him to miss the stimulating presence of those he had known there. Certainly he was not resentful that his wife was the star attraction in Florence and Paris, for there was no jealousy in him. He visibly worshiped Elizabeth and always praised her poetry far above his own. Biographers who have attempted to prove that Robert Browning regretted his marriage have read meanings into poems like "Andrea del Sarto" that were never intended. If there was one thing about which he was and had been completely sure, it was the rightness of his marriage.

He was definitely concerned about his son. Pen, he knew, was badly spoiled, and met all attempts at discipline with temper tantrums. The child was also very adept at getting his own way, especially from his mother, and there seemed to be no way to convince Elizabeth that her indulgence would ultimately do Pen no good. Also, it was a great worry to him that his own work was not prospering. He had realized that he had been for some time finding it increasingly difficult to write. The introduction to Shelley's letters had recalled his early devotion to the "sun-treader," a devotion which time had only increased. In maturity he appreciated Shelley's genius even more than he had as a boy. And Shelley had made his name as a great poet by the time he was thirty. Robert Browning was forty, and the public recognition he had hoped for was still as remote as it had been nineteen years ago, when he wrote *Pauline*.

It was in this mood that he sat alone on a gloomy afternoon in January, 1852, to fulfill his stint of one poem a day. When he left his desk, he had completed that strangely evocative work, "Childe Roland to the Dark Tower Came." This poem has been torn to shreds in search of its meaning, but it seems obvious that this narrative of the Would-be Knight, who is in quest of that mysterious dark tower, "After a life spent training for the sight," who wonders only, "should I be fit?" even for failure, is the story of the poet's own quest for the inspiration that will bring clearness of vision and the fulfillment of his vow to poetry. Significantly enough, the horrors that greet Childe Roland's eyes as he follows the road across the gray plain, the "safe road" having vanished from sight—horrors such as the spavined, blind horse, the rusty war machine, the mysterious evidence of a bitter battle with no footsteps leading in or out of the "horrid mews" where it had taken place, the slimy river, the "palsied oak"—none of these things has any power to hurt him except in his own imagination. It is his conjectures about them that make him tremble with fear, not their objective reality. Then, just as he despairs of ever reaching the Dark Tower, it looms up before his sight. But now, though he is still afraid, he casts these fears from him.

> . . . noise was everywhere! it tolled
>   Increasing like a bell. Names in my ears,
>   Of all the lost adventurers my peers,—
> How such a one was strong, and such was bold,
> And such was fortunate, yet each of old
>   Lost, lost! One moment knelled the woe of years.
>
> There they stood, ranged along the hillsides, met
>   To view the last of me, a living frame
>   For one more picture! In a sheet of flame
> I saw them and I knew them all. And yet
> Dauntless the slug-horn to my lips I set,
>   And blew. *"Childe Roland to the Dark Tower came."*

Just as Robert Browning had exorcised his religious doubts by writing *Christmas Eve and Easter Day,* so in "Childe Roland to the Dark Tower Came" he apparently settled the question of his own creative quest. Immediate success or failure did not matter. The important thing was to continue, to reach the Dark Tower, to search for truth no matter what torturing way the search led; then, having found it, dauntless as Childe Roland even in the face of seeming disaster, to "set the slug-horn to [one's] lips and blow."

All that winter and spring he worked steadily. In July, 1852, he took Elizabeth and Pen to England, where his presence was urgently needed. His father was involved in a breach-of-promise suit, and the legal complications were endless. Between conferences with attorneys, Browning did manage to see his many friends and to make a number of new ones. John Ruskin invited him to lunch; he met Charles Kingsley whose ideas on Christian Socialism were attracting as much attention as his novels. Dante Gabriel Rossetti came to call, bringing with him all the enthusiasm that the Pre-Raphaelite Brotherhood expressed for Robert Browning's poetry. James Russell Lowell was in London that summer and he came with his wife to pay his respects to the Brownings. Mrs. Carlyle appeared with Mazzini in tow. Mazzini was once more an exile, but still full of plans for the liberation of Italy. An unexpected pleasure was a visit from Florence Nightingale, who was struggling to find some way to study nursing; and the most delightful and unusual occasion was the christening of Alfred Tennyson's son, Hallam. Elizabeth was not well enough to attend, but Browning, who attended more or less reluctantly at her insistence, returned home in high fettle, announcing that he had held the baby for ten minutes, actually, and the baby had not cried!

Late in September, the senior Mr. Browning's case came to court. Because of some indiscreet letters he had written which were introduced in evidence, the judgment went against him. His lawyers urged an appeal, but the *Times* had already published a detailed account of the trial, and his son shrank from any more unpleasant publicity than the family had already received. It was considered advisable that Mr. Browning be away from England for a while, and, fortunately, he was persuaded to follow this advice. Browning helped him and Sariana to find an apartment in Paris, and the entire family was in that city on the day that, true to his prediction, Louis Napoleon made his triumphal entry as emperor of France.

Having seen his father and sister comfortably settled for the time being, Browning returned to Florence with Elizabeth and Pen and settled down to work in earnest. "I have not left the house one evening since our return," he wrote Joseph Milsand, the French critic, on February 24, 1853. "I am writing—a first step towards popularity for me—lyrics with more music and painting than before, so as to get people to hear and see. . . ." [8] This is the first hint of his new collection, which was to emerge as *Men and Women*.

Summer found him still at work at Bagni di Lucca, but by autumn of 1853 he was ready for a change, so the household moved to Rome. The day after their arrival, Elizabeth was thrown into complete panic by the death of William Wetmore Storey's little boy of gastric fever. (Storey, an American sculptor, and his wife had spent the summer at Bagni di Lucca and were now wintering in Rome.) She was terrified lest Pen fall ill, too, and wanted to leave Rome at once; but her husband persuaded her to stay, and nothing worse happened to Pen that winter than a few stomach upsets from too many children's parties.

The shock of the Storey tragedy, however, brought on a recurrence of Elizabeth's nervous attacks, so she was obliged to spend a considerable amount of time resting. Browning, however, went out a great many evenings. Thackeray was in Rome, and so were Fanny Kemble and her sister Mrs. Sartoris, whose ability as a singer was much admired. John Lockhart, the critic and editor of the *Quarterly Review*, met Browning at a party and later paid him the highest compliment of which his Scots forthrightness was capable: "He isn't at all like a damned literary man!" [4]

Browning continued to work steadily all that winter, however, despite the distractions of Rome, and for the entire year following at Florence. The schedule was broken only for Pen's lessons. Elizabeth listened to him read for an hour each morning before beginning work on *Aurora Leigh,* and Browning gave him a piano lesson before starting on his day's stint. Sometimes in the late afternoon they would receive callers or pay visits. Frederick Tennyson, the poet laureate's brother, who had a villa nearby, often made the charming gesture of hiring an entire symphony orchestra to entertain his guests, and the Brownings were frequently present at his musical evenings. Browning did take time to read the newspaper accounts of the Crimean War, which made him furious, but for the most part he lived in the immediate world about him and with the men and women of his own creation. Fra Lippo Lippi, Andrea del Sarto, Bishop Blougram, Galuppi Baldassare—husbands, wives, happy and disappointed lovers—these filled his mind and heart. As he finished each poem, he sent it to his publisher in London, and Elizabeth stopped work on *Aurora Leigh* to help him read proof. By June, 1855, the last word was written, but he added a final poem—"One Word More. To E.B.B.":

There they are, my fifty men and women
Naming me the fifty poems finished!
Take then, Love, the book and me together:
Where the heart lies, let the brain be also.

Men and Women was thereby made his ardent return tribute to the poet of *Sonnets from the Portuguese*.

A few days after the final corrected proofs were dispatched, they left Florence for London—Browning to see his book through the press, and Elizabeth to make another futile attempt to see her father. The usual social festivities attended their visits; two evenings were especially eventful. One was the occasion when Tennyson and Rossetti spent an evening with the Brownings. Tennyson recited all of his poem "Maud," and Browning, not to be outdone, recited "Fra Lippo Lippi." Rossetti did not recite; he contented himself with sketching, but the presence of three major poets under the same roof at the same moment was sufficient to throw Elizabeth into ecstasies. It is doubtful that a more unique performance—for contemporary accounts testify that both men were accomplished readers who definitely acted their poems as well as recited them— has ever been recorded.

The second occasion was just as memorable, but not at all pleasant. It involved the one disagreement in the Browning marriage—spiritualism. Spiritualism was a current craze. People flocked to the theatre to see demonstrations and tried their hands at seances and table-tipping. Even Queen Victoria was discreetly interested in it. Elizabeth had become deeply involved shortly after her marriage, and she had taken part in seances at Florence. Browning, though he scoffed at the whole idea of psychic phenomena, could understand the attraction that spiritualism held for his wife. Elizabeth, he knew, had never completely reconciled herself to her brother's tragic death at

Torquay, and in spiritualism she was seeking for more tangible evidence of an afterlife than religion gave her. If she could convince herself that "Bro" was truly happy, she would feel less guilty. So Browning did not interfere, even though he was frequently exasperated by the talk he heard in his drawing room in Florence when Elizabeth entertained friends who were as ardent believers as she.

The most celebrated medium of the day was a Scots-born American clairvoyant, Daniel Dunglas Home. He had already astonished New York and Boston, and in the summer of 1855 was showing his extraordinary powers in London. Elizabeth was eager to meet him, and Browning was curious about him, too. Through Mrs. Jameson they met a Mr. and Mrs. Rymer, who invited them to an informal gathering at their home in Ealing, promising that Home would be present and conduct a seance. When the Brownings arrived, Home showed them a wreath of white clematis which the Rymer daughters had made, and told them that "spirit hands" would remove the wreath from the center of the table and place it on Elizabeth's head. The room was darkened and the seance proceeded. The wreath seemingly was pushed from the table, but from this moment on, accounts of the episode differ. Browning maintained later that the wreath had been passed to him under the table. Elizabeth insisted that it was indeed placed on her head by a large hand, "white as snow." Both accounts agree that the room was by then too dark to see clearly, so it was impossible for anyone but Mr. Home to know exactly what did happen. Then the table tilted and there was a sound of music like an accordian, and Home went into a trance, speaking in a voice which the Rymers said they recognized as that of their child who had died three years earlier. By that time, Browning was convinced that the whole affair was a fraud. He asked that the "spirit hand" return so that he could see it, but the Rymers would not permit the medium to be disturbed. Elizabeth, of course, was entirely convinced, and kept the wreath.

Several days later, Browning had brought himself to a state of such dissatisfaction that he requested Mrs. Rymer to permit him to view another seance, but this was refused. To him, refusal was tantamount to an admission that Home was indeed a fake, and when the Rymers came to call, bringing Home with them, he refused the medium's proffered hand. Instead he vehemently expressed his disapproval and disbelief. Home demanded to speak in his own defense, and Browning, pale with anger, demanded that he be silent. During the altercation, Elizabeth stood wringing her hands, lamenting over and over, "Dear Mr. Home, I am not to blame! Oh, dear! Oh, dear!" Finally the Rymers and Home departed, leaving Elizabeth in a state of near collapse, and Browning in a state of remorse for having upset her, but, all the same, feeling less worried at having spoken his mind in what he felt was protection of her. The wilted wreath he tossed out of the window, and doubtless wished he could dispose of his wife's interest in spiritualism that easily. But in points of belief, she was as strong-willed as he, and when occasion arose she continued to discuss spiritualism with her friends, but no longer in his presence. Only several years later, when she was cruelly deceived by one of these friends was she willing to admit, most reluctantly, that she had been duped, and that her husband, when he had stamped on the floor in a rage protesting her gullibility, had been right. It was at this time that Browning wrote "Mr. Sludge, 'The Medium,' " later published in *Dramatis Personae,* a dramatic monologue in which a fraudulent medium exposes his chicanery. But this was one poem that he did not show to Elizabeth.

In October, 1855, the Brownings returned to Paris, there to await publication of *Men and Women*. Browning had put all the creative strength and power he possessed into this book and was counting heavily on it to make his reputation. But this was not to be. The poems—some of the greatest he ever wrote, such as "Andrea del Sarto," "Fra Lippo Lippi," "Bishop Blougram's Apology," "Childe Roland," "The Last Ride Together"—were denounced for obscurity and unpleasantness. The public, caught up in the frenzy of the Crimean War, did not want to read even "A Woman's Last Word," which tells so perceptively and beautifully of the delicate adjustments necessary in marriage, nor of the joy of life proclaimed so exultantly in "Saul." Dante Gabriel Rossetti liked the book, and William Morris reviewed it enthusiastically for the *Oxford and Cambridge Magazine*. The rest of the reviewers were hostile at worst and condescending at best. Robert Browning had reached his Dark Tower, only to find that his horn was mute.

8

The next six years of Robert Browning's life were marked by little or no writing. In the months immediately following October, 1855, work seemed impossible for him. Even the debacle of *Sordello* had not overwhelmed him as much as the failure of *Men and Women* to find its audience, and, while he did not brood over that failure, his intellectual conviction that the achievement of success was not as important as the performance of the task could not conquer his emotional and spiritual depression. He tried by every means he knew to revive the inspiration that had always been so magnificently resilient in the preceding years. He helped Elizabeth to revise and proofread *Aurora Leigh,* and no one was more delighted at its immediate success when it was published in 1856 than he; he tried, at her suggestion, to revise *Sordello.* He verified some information for Thomas Carlyle who was working on a biography of Emperor Frederick the Great; he took up drawing and clay-modeling, went to museums and art exhibits, attended concerts, read constantly, but nothing seemed to help. All else went by the board against the ever constant nagging thought at the back of his mind that he was forty-four years old and had failed at the one thing he most wanted. He was still living on his wife's income, despite his brave promises—though as far as Elizabeth was concerned, he was a complete success in the promise she counted first: his love and care for her. She grieved for his disappointment. He was her world. That he did not succumb to complete bitterness and despair was and is a tribute to his own strength of character, deeply convinced faith, and fundamental common sense; but he suffered only as an artist deprived of inspiration can suffer. He could not know, and would probably have laughed at the idea, that he was ahead of his time.

And he had other griefs to bear. John Kenyon, who had become his devoted friend, as well as Elizabeth's, died in December, 1856. Kenyon left both of them large individual legacies in his will—a demonstration of affection and confidence that touched Robert Browning deeply and was of great material assistance, but his friend's death was a shattering loss. No other man had been as close to him, no one else had been as quietly understanding and reassuring. Then, in April, 1857, Mr. Barrett died, obdurate to the last. Elizabeth, prostrated by the news, became desperately ill. Browning took her to Bagni di Lucca, in hope that the change and the mountain air would be beneficial as it had been in the past, but she had made only a little progress when Pen became ill with the dreaded gastric fever, and she had a relapse. Both had to be nursed around the clock; Isa Blagden, who fortunately was also vacationing at Bagni di Lucca, practically moved in with them and was of inestimable help. They returned to Florence in October, to experience one of the coldest winters Italy had ever known. There was no possibility of going anywhere else; Elizabeth simply was not able to travel, and Rome, even Naples, were no warmer. By the spring of 1858, they were all physically and emotionally depleted. The warmer weather revived Browning's spirit, however, with good effect on Elizabeth. She became well enough at last to receive visitors, among them Nathaniel Hawthorne and his wife, and, later, William Cullen Bryant, when they called to pay homage to the author of *Aurora Leigh*. Hawthorne and Browning liked each other immediately; for one thing, they both agreed that Daniel Dunglas Home was indeed a fraud! Hawthorne recorded in his notebook that Browning was a brilliant conversationalist—"even his nonsense was of very genuine and excellent quality, the true babble and effervescence of a bright and powerful mind." [1] The friendship between them continued until the American novelist's death in 1864, and it was Robert Browning whom Una Hawthorne asked for help in preparing her father's last novel, *Septimus Felton,* for posthumous publication.

The Brownings spent the winter of 1858-59 in Rome, where Robert Browning found himself much in demand socially. "So, plenty of distractions and no 'Men and Women,' " [2] Elizabeth wrote regretfully to Isa Blagden. She had rather the attention were given to the author of *Men and Women,* but since all the invitations naturally included her, and she was not strong enough to attend large balls and receptions, her husband was, in a sense, representing the author of *Aurora Leigh.* In March, 1859, the Prince of Wales visited Rome, and Browning was invited to meet him. The chief topic of conversation was the revival of the Risorgimento, and the help that Emperor Louis Napoleon had promised to give the Italian cause. It was generally recognized that Louis Napoleon had his own reasons for this promise, given secretly to Count Cavour who was now the leader of the revolt. The French Emperor wanted to humble Austria, but Italians nevertheless looked upon him as their savior, and the Italian battle hymn, "Vittoria," alternated with the "Marseillaise" in the streets. The promised French assistance made the Italian armies bold enough to strike a firm blow for freedom and independence; when the Brownings returned to Florence in May, they found that Grand Duke Ferdinand had fled, and that the city had declared itself for a united Italy under Victor Emmanuel, son of Charles Albert, that king of Sardinia who had led the army of revolution in the forties.

The combined armies of Italy and France met the Austrian army near Magenta in Lombardy, on June 4, 1859, and Austria was compelled to retreat. They met again at Solferino on June 24, and once again the Allies were victorious. Then, just as it seemed as though Louis Napoleon's promise to liberate Italy from the Alps to the Adriatic would be fulfilled, the French Emperor asked for an armistice. On July 11, he met with Emperor Franz Joseph of Austria at Villafranca to draw up a peace treaty. The overwhelming disillusionment that swept Italy was as violent as the former enthusiasm. Louis Napoleon was denounced as vigorously as he had formerly been praised. Robert Browning, watching the proceedings, said that his original impression of the man was only the more confirmed. Elizabeth, who had been wildly partisan, became acutely ill. She would accept no explanation of Louis Napoleon's perfidy on political or military grounds; neither would she blame him. She was convinced that fear on the part of other nations, especially England, of what a united Italy might do to the balance of power in Europe, had forced him to sign a treaty when victory seemed within his grasp.

Her illness was so desperate that her physician feared that she was having an attack of angina. He positively ordered Robert Browning to get her out of Florence immediately and into quieter surroundings, and he even followed them to Siena, to make certain that his orders were being obeyed. Her strength was never so slow in returning, but by autumn she felt that she was able to make the journey to Rome. She was working on a new volume, *Poems before Congress,* and talked of nothing but politics.

Browning tried to make her rest and to be as quiet as possible, but he knew as no one else could how deeply her emotions were involved in the Italian cause, and, for the first time in their marriage, he was afraid for her. She was very frail; yet she was literally burning herself out in talking and writing, trying to tell the world what the revolution really meant. Harriet Beecher Stowe came to see her, and they talked about the American slavery issue—and about spiritualism, in which Mrs. Stowe was a devout believer. Her visit left Elizabeth exhausted, but she scoffed affectionately at her husband's remonstrances. All his pleas for rest and quiet had little effect, and he welcomed with relief the visits of Theodore Parker, the celebrated American clergyman, who was wintering in Rome in a vain attempt to recover his health. Though he was a liberal, his political comments were not upsetting to her, and Elizabeth found great spiritual comfort in his conversations.

Though the Risorgimento was officially over, the struggle was continuing, and a new name was on everyone's lips—Garibaldi. Garibaldi, veteran of Custoza, had raised an army, "The Thousand"—the exact number was one thousand and eighty nine—and was planning an attack, some said on Sicily, some on Naples, and some on Rome itself. The atmosphere was tense with apprehension, for what could an inexperienced red-shirted company, made up of doctors, teachers, lawyers, engineers, and storekeepers, do against the proved might of Austria? Garibaldi was given one chance in a thousand to succeed. Then, on May 14, 1860, he and his Thousand landed in Sicily and entered the town of Marsala. Within an hour it was in his hands, and he had ordered his army, swelled by hundreds of new recruits, to advance on Messina.

Elizabeth was exhilarated and happy over this victory, and her health immediately seemed considerably improved.

Browning took her to Siena for the summer, and by autumn she had apparently recovered completely. Word of her sister Henrietta's illness shadowed her exhilaration over Garibaldi's continued success, though she took some satisfaction in the news that the English people, if not their government, had realized the gravity of the Italian cause, and that a company of English volunteers would soon be fighting beside the Italian troops. But she was deeply concerned for Henrietta; she had a foreboding that she was not being told the entire truth, and soon after she and her husband reached Rome in November, a letter arrived which confirmed her worst fears. Henrietta had died of cancer.

Browning, himself deeply grieved because he had been very fond of Henrietta Barrett, had to acknowledge the letters of condolence because Elizabeth was too ill to do so. During the entire winter she was a complete invalid; she went nowhere and saw very few visitors. But she continued to read the newspapers avidly, and when she was strong enough she wrote letters about Italian politics to family and friends. Now all her hopes were centered on Count Cavour, who seemed to her the best and noblest of men. Browning, too, felt optimistic about Cavour's attempts to make Italy a real nation, even against the enormous odds that faced him, and since he was more emotionally detached from the situation, he could view it more objectively. Garibaldi, for instance, was a good soldier and a crafty strategist, but as member of a parliament he was a disaster. Browning saw, too, that a country which had lived so long in disunity and under a foreign power, would not soon be able to establish itself as a united, independent nation.

He did not discuss the matter with Elizabeth. Her emotions were at fever pitch and her health was too precarious. Besides, he had assumed complete responsibility for Pen's education, and that kept him fully occupied. It was almost impossible to make the boy concentrate on his studies, and his work was not up to the standard that an English school would demand of an eleven-year-old. Browning was by turns worried, exasperated, and enraged. The kind of camaraderie he had enjoyed with his own father was quite impossible, for Pen seemed to lack all intellectual curiosity. The boy had, of course, been affected by his mother's many illnesses and by his never having been sent to school, so Browning tried to be patient, even though patience with children was not one of his salient characteristics, as he was aware. But there seemed to be no way to cope with such adamant resistance to learning, and the task was doubly difficult because Elizabeth insisted that no one must be "too hard" on Pen. Frequently, after a stormy morning of lessons, Browning fled to the studio of William Wetmore Storey, where he relaxed by modeling clay. Working with clay was no substitute for a poem, but at least it was a way to work off the tension engendered by a determined, sulky, rebellious little boy.

Early in the spring of 1861, since Elizabeth was apparently so much better, Browning enthusiastically proposed that they take a real summer holiday and go to Fontainebleau, where his father and sister, and her sister Arabel, might join them. Elizabeth was equally enthusiastic. She felt that she had gained a considerable amount of strength during her restful winter in Rome; indeed, she had been well enough to receive Hans Christian Andersen when he came to pay his respects. But a week before they were scheduled to leave, she had an attack of asthma and pulmonary congestion. Browning, over her protests, canceled the French holiday, and they went instead to Florence, intending to go on within a few weeks to Siena or Bagni di Lucca. Elizabeth seemed no more exhausted than usual after the comparatively short journey from Rome to Casa Guidi, so Browning was not unduly anxious. But when Count Cavour suddenly died at Milan on June 6, Elizabeth mourned as one personally bereaved, and her grief and agitation brought on another violent asthmatic attack. She had hardly realized herself how deeply she loved her adopted country. All she had really known of England was the one room in the Wimpole Street house. Her real life had commenced, she always avowed, with her love for Robert Browning and his for her, and her love was the greater because he had not insisted upon their returning to England to live under the shadow of her father's anger. Italy was her home, and now she wept over Italy's loss of the one man who seemed strong enough to make a nation out of chaos.

After a few days, however, she rallied, and she did not permit the visitors who were admitted to see or know how truly ill she was. Especially because of the anxiety it would cause him, she did not permit her husband to realize her condition. He was so happy to think her better that he was unaware of the extent of her weakness. The weather that June was treacherous, alternating between scorching heat and sudden cold, and Casa Guidi was drafty. Late that month she caught a cold and coughed so much that the doctor gravely informed Browning that he suspected an abscess in one of her lungs. Browning was frantic, but Elizabeth scoffed at him, saying humorously that she knew this was only one of her usual attacks and that she would be better soon. But she grew steadily weaker. Every day Browning had to carry her from her bed to the drawing-room sofa, where she insisted upon reading the papers. He tried to persuade her to eat, but she could swallow nothing but broth. Still she insisted that she was better. Isa Blagden came to visit her on the evening of June 28, and Elizabeth animatedly discussed the new Italian prime minister, whom she hoped would carry out Cavour's policies. Isa reasssured Browning as she left; surely if Elizabeth was able to speak in such a fashion, without a trace of a cough, she must indeed be feeling stronger.

Browning, nevertheless, sat all night by her bed, troubled by her uneven sleep. When she would awaken, she would smile gratefully. At three o'clock in the morning, noticing that her hands and feet were like ice, he became alarmed. He sent the porter to fetch the doctor, and told Wilson, who was still with them, to bring some hot water. Carefully he raised Elizabeth and seated her on the edge of the bed, so that she might put her feet in a basin. "Well," she said smiling, "you do make an exaggerated case of it." Browning bathed her hands with hot water and tried to make her drink some hot broth. When she could not raise the cup herself, he fed the liquid to her by the teaspoonful. When she had taken all that she could swallow, he put the cup and spoon aside, and sat on the bed beside her, holding her in his arms. Suddenly she put her arms tightly around his neck and kissed him, whispering brokenly how much she loved him—how she had always loved him, and always would. Browning, loath to let her go, but fearing what the slightest exertion might do, gently eased her back on her pillows and replaced the blankets. "Are you comfortable?" he asked gently. "Beautiful," she answered smilingly, and closed her eyes. Browning spoke softly to her and she continued smiling, and then—

> . . . I saw. I felt she must be raised and took her in my arms—I felt the struggle to cough begin, and end unavailingly—no pain, no sigh, only a quiet *sight*— her head fell on me.[3]

Isa Blagden came next morning and spent the day at Casa Guidi, returning to her villa late that evening with Pen. The next day, Monday, June 30, all the shops in the Casa Guidi section were closed, as Florentines mourned their loss. That evening, after a graveside service, Elizabeth Barrett Browning was buried in the Protestant Cemetery, and her husband returned to Casa Guidi alone.

His grief was profound. His sense of desolation and loneliness was overwhelming. As he said later, "My heart is buried in Italy." But he could feel no rebellion. There was only gratitude for the fifteen years of complete happiness that he had known with Elizabeth. He had been fortunate as few men were; he had been permitted to experience the giving and receiving of a love that many would never know, no matter how long they lived. That love would be his strength.

But he could not remain in Florence. There were too many reminders of a past which, though inexpressibly dear, was now past. Better to go to fresh surroundings, where the memories of those fifteen years would not be so vividly associated with particular sights, particular streets, a particular house where Elizabeth had always been to greet him, a sun-lit piazza at midday, a bridge over a quiet river looming black in the moonlight. That he and Elizabeth would meet again, he had no doubt.

> For sudden the worst turns the best to the brave,
> The black minute's at end,
> And the elements' rage, the fiend-voices that rave,
> Shall dwindle, shall blend,
> Shall change, shall become first a peace out of pain,
> Then a light, then thy breast,
> Oh thou soul of my soul! I shall clasp thee again,
> And with God be the rest.

The past was gone, the future was in God's hands, but the present was now, and he must live in the present. There was Pen to think of, a bewildered twelve-year old boy, far less mature than most boys his age, who wept at everything and nothing, who only dimly understood his own loss and could not begin to comprehend that of his father. Pen was now Robert Browning's sole responsibility and Pen must be his first concern. With his characteristic energy, once a decision was made, he prepared to leave Italy. Casa Guidi was dismantled and the furniture put in storage. Pen was taken to the barber for a haircut and to the tailor for an English schoolboy's suit. On August 1, 1861, all was ready. With only the briefest backward glance, Browning left Florence, never to return.

9

Isa Blagden traveled with them as far as Paris. Browning had thought of spending some time there with his father and sister, but, after twenty-four hours, the noisy city became unbearable. He needed a quiet place where no demands would be made upon him, and his family understandingly agreed. Within a few days, Browning, his father and sister, Pen, and Pen's pony riding in the baggage car in its own box stall, were aboard a train for St. Egabert in Brittany. Several weeks later he wrote to Isa, who had remained in Paris, saying that "it was the best place I could have gone to." [1] Their seaside villa was quiet, the air was marvelous, and the natives had never heard the names of either Robert or Elizabeth Barrett Browning. He devoted his time to getting better acquainted with his son, taking him for walks along the beach, swimming with him in the surf, watching him ride, and giving his critical opinion of the sketches and water colors which Pen turned out daily under his grandfather's tutelage. Gradually he emerged from his state of shock. By September he forced himself to plan for spending the winter in London, and he wrote to William Wetmore Storey that he was "impatient at doing nothing."

His father and sister returned to Paris in October, and he and Pen began their journey to England. There was a most exasperating contretemps at the railway station when the authorities refused to take the pony aboard. Browning wore down their resistance after two hours' argument, but, since there was no such thing as a through train, the pony had to be transferred at every stop. "I am kept till the last before he [the pony] can be gotten at, and reach hotels an hour after my party," [2] he wrote ruefully to Isa Blagden. He was learning quickly that being the father of a twelve-year-old made for complications that had been hitherto unsuspected.

Once in London, he was faced with the task of finding a place to live. He had determined that he would never again establish a home—home was Casa Guidi. A furnished apartment in Westbourne Terrace which was near Isa Blagden's London residence seemed the best solution, so he took a lease. Within a few months, however, he found lodgings impossible. He was too accustomed to the freedom of his own home to be happy with anything else. While Pen embarked on his studies with a tutor, Browning went house hunting, and at last found 19 Warwick Crescent, near the Grand Junction Canal. The surroundings reminded him somewhat of Venice, particularly the bridge spanning the canal just beyond the house and the little island of trees which he could see from the upstairs windows. He sent to Florence for his furniture, which seemed to arrange itself to make the rooms look very much like Casa Guidi. Surprisingly, he found it a comfort to see Elizabeth's chair before the fireplace, opposite his own. Surrounded by the things which were part of the life they both had loved, he found his own desolation easier to bear.

His first and foremost concern was, of course, Pen. He was determined that Pen must go to Oxford. The restrictions which had prevented his own entrance at Oxford had been relaxed, so there was no reason why his son should not take a university degree. But Pen's education had been so haphazard that entering him in a public school was not to be thought of. Eton, Harrow, Winchester, Rugby—none would have accepted him, ill prepared as he was. So a tutor was engaged to keep Pen at his Greek and Latin, and his father hoped for the best. Patience and gentle insistence, he was certain, would transform Pen into a model English school boy. "Don't fear . . . I shall never become a 'monomaniac' about Pen's education," he wrote to Isa Blagden in March, 1862. "I made an effort because it was wanted . . . Had I made less, he would have gained less." [3] He added proudly that, after six months in England, Pen's disposition was now all that anyone could wish, and that an hour's rowing every day on the canal was doing wonders for his health.

Apart from Pen, Browning's principal occupation was preparing Elizabeth's last poems for publication. This work he considered even more important than readying the new edition of his own *Collected Works* which had been announced for 1863. He went out socially very little that first winter in London, preferring to spend his leisure time with his son. When Thackeray retired from the editorship of the *Cornhill Magazine* early in 1862, Browning was immediately offered the position, but he declined appreciatively, saying that Pen and his editing kept him fully occupied. The only diversions he permitted himself were the regular Sunday morning service at Bedford Chapel, and a daily afternoon call upon Arabel Barrett, whose philanthropic work with destitute girls greatly interested him. It would have interested Elizabeth too, he thought. She would have applauded Arabel.

Every day in this year 1862 he became more fully aware of the great changes that had come to England during his fifteen years away. Queen Victoria, who used to appear so frequently among her admiring subjects, had secluded herself in Windsor Castle, mourning the death of her husband, Albert, the Prince Consort. What would have been thought impossible fifteen years ago had happened: a Jew, Benjamin Disraeli, was a rising power in the House of Commons, though he was being challenged by the leader of the liberal opposition, William Gladstone. A short, brutal war in India had brought that country firmly under English control. Charles Darwin's *Origin of Species* had been published in 1859, rocking religious orthodoxy to its foundations. The first trans-Atlantic cable for carrying telegraph messages between England and America had been attempted. Reform bills to widen the franchise and to make education a state concern were in the making. And the people of Ireland, still seething over England's neglect in the terrible 1845 famine, continued in a constant state of eruption and rebellion.

There had been changes in the literary world as well. A host of new names now clamored for recognition. Dickens had just published *Great Expectations*, but his novels now vied with those of Anthony Trollope, Charles Reade, and George Eliot. Tennyson had published four of his *Idylls of the King* and was secure on his laureate's pedestal, but he was being challenged by Matthew Arnold, Dante Gabriel Rossetti, and William Morris. In a few years, a most uninhibited young man named Algernon Swinburne would devastate the reading public with his *Atalanta in Calydon,* as Edward FitzGerald had already done with his *Rubaiyat.* Carlyle was still writing; John Stuart Mill's essay *On Liberty* had caused a great furore in philosophical and political circles.

Robert Browning, always attuned to the climate of opinion wherever he lived, was gradually caught up in this intellectual and creative ferment. He knew about the Pre-Raphaelite painters but had not yet viewed their work; in January, 1862, he surprised Rossetti by paying two visits to his studio. He dined quietly with John Ruskin, now considered the leading art critic in London, and discussed painting with him. He called on George Eliot, despite the disapproval of his more conventional friends over her liaison with George Henry Lewes, and told Isa Blagden that he liked them both! The company of other writers stimulated him, and slowly he began to feel the need again to put his own thoughts on paper. He spent the summer of 1862 with Pen at St. Marie in Brittany, but by autumn he remarked that he felt like a sparrow in a cage. In October, he returned to London, refreshed and eager to begin work on a new volume.

The next eighteen months passed quickly. Browning spent most of his time at his desk, but there are glimpses of him at dinner parties and at balls. Pen, at fourteen, was receiving invitations to evening parties, but tutoring limited his contacts with young people his own age and he did not like to attend these alone. So his father always was persuaded to accompany him and found that the "adult accompanying guests," as they humorously termed themselves, usually made a most lively and interesting little group. In a letter to Isa Blagden, Browning amusingly recorded William Gladstone's loud discussion of the relative merits of *Romola* and *Wuthering Heights*, and said that he disagreed with that gentleman's opinion of both novels! He himself had not enjoyed *Romola*, but felt that *Wuthering Heights* had a "certain grandeur." He took time to read Ernest Renan's rationalistic *Life of Jesus* and found its thesis very weak. At one of the adult parties he met Garibaldi, who was soliciting funds for his cause in England. This was at the American embassy where, he said, one always met interesting people. He was in London when the Prince of Wales married Princess Alexandra of Denmark in March, 1863, and went to see the illuminations with Charles Dickens. He visited his father in Paris briefly that spring, and took Pen to Brittany again in August. But his writing continued on absolute schedule, and when he returned to London in autumn, *Dramatis Personae* was ready for publication.

The book appeared in May, 1864. To his intense delight, it sold out quickly and a second edition—his first—was called for that same year. He was further pleased by the news that many copies were being sold at Oxford and Cambridge, indicating that the younger generation was reading his poetry. The critics, too, were most cordial. Many who had damned *Men and Women* out of hand in 1855 were now ready for *Dramatis Personae* and hailed the work as a major achievement. Browning's poetry in those nine intervening years had found an audience in the younger readers who had learned from Ruskin and Rossetti to appreciate Italy, who had read Carlyle and Mill and understood their pleas for liberty of thought and conscience, who had recognized in Darwin's scientific treatise the same theories that *Paracelsus* had unscientifically advanced, and who, above all, understood what the poet was attempting to do when he made his men and women speak. They enjoyed the exposed hypocrisy of "Mr. Sludge, 'The Medium' " and the satire on the evolutionists in "Caliban upon Setebos." They had been bombarded by the new Biblical criticism, and so could appreciate "A Death in the Desert" which attacked the then (also) current theory that John the Evangelist did not write the Fourth Gospel. Rabbi ben Ezra's praise of old age,

> Grow old along with me!
> The best is yet to be,
> The last of life for which the first was made.

was an inspiring answer to voices of doom which said that old age was to be feared by the young. *Dramatis Personae* was a remarkable example of Browning's ability to make poetry out of current issues by putting them into historical perspective, which permitted him to remove controversies from their emotional contemporary contexts. The crowning glory of the volume, however, was, and is, "Abt Vogler." In it, the great organist-improvisateur speaks longingly of his desire to give permanence to his art, and his solution,

> On the earth, the broken arcs; in the heaven, a perfect round.

is Browning's own belief. In *Christmas Eve and Easter Day* he had said that the artist's creation was only a reflection of God's creation; in "Andrea del Sarto," he had cried, "Ah, but a man's reach should exceed his grasp, or what's a heaven for?" No one could hope for perfection on this earth, but one must attempt it even in the face of great odds. The attempt was man's obligation; the extent of his actual accomplishment would be known when he faced his Creator.

Greatly cheered and encouraged, Browning took Pen abroad in August, this time to Cambo in the Pyrenees. In September he went to Biarritz, where he wrote Isa Blagden,

> For me, I have got on by having a great read at Euripides, the one book I brought with me, besides attending to my own matters, my new poem that is about to be; and of which the whole is pretty well in my head—the Roman murder story of which you know.[4]

This is the first mention of *The Ring and the Book,* the gigantic work which was to occupy him completely for the next four years.

Actually, his interest in the "Roman murder story" considerably antedated his letter to Isa Blagden. In June, 1860, on a bookstall in Florence, he had come upon a vellum-covered volume, partly printed and partly in manuscript, "The Old Yellow Book," which was a transcript of the trial of an Italian nobleman for the murder of his wife in 1689. At that very moment, he had seen the possibilities of the story, but he did not begin work on it. Some biographers have indicated that Elizabeth had found the subject distasteful and that he had deferred to her wishes, but this reasoning seems a little improbable. After all, Elizabeth's own *Aurora Leigh* is quite as dramatic in its way as *The Ring and the Book* and deals with subject matter quite as "realistic." It is more likely that the revolutionary excitement of 1860, combined with his great concern over Elizabeth's health, had made embarking on a long, sustained project impossible. Then, her death in 1861 had shattered his world. But by autumn, 1864, he had picked up the threads of his life again, certain that this was what Elizabeth would have wished. With the success of *Dramatis Personae* behind him and the new edition of his *Collected Works* selling well, he had the inspiration and energy to devote to what he now knew must be his major work.

The story given in "The Old Yellow Book" in cut-and-dried legal prose was a sordid one. Guido Franceschini, an impoverished, dissolute nobleman of Arezzo, had married Pompilia Comparini, assuming that she was an heiress. He discovered shortly after marriage that her wealth was not what her parents had led him to believe, and further, that the Comparini had concealed the fact that she was an illegitimate foundling whom they had adopted. Guido vented his fury most cruelly upon his young wife, who submitted for four years, until she discovered that she was going to have a child. In desperation, she turned to the

one person who could help her if he could be persuaded—
Giuseppe Caponsacchi, a young, handsome priest. Caponsacchi, touched by her innocence and righteously angered
by the suffering she had so long endured, agreed to take
her to her "parents" in Rome. Guido, her husband, followed, caught them about fifteen miles from Rome, and
had them arrested as adulterers. Caponsacchi was tried and
sentenced to ecclesiastical discipline. Pompilia was sent to
a convent; but, because of her condition, she was soon re-
leased under bond to the Comparini and under protection
of the law returned to their home to have her child.

A few weeks after the baby was born, Guido came to
Rome with four of his henchmen, and tricked Pompilia
into opening the door by saying that he carried a message
from Caponsacchi. The five assassins killed Pietro and
Violante Comparini, and left Pompilia dying of twenty-
two stab wounds. Guido was caught, tried for murder, con-
demned, and sentenced to death. Because he had at one
time taken minor orders in the Church, he appealed the
sentence to the pope. The pope, however, refused clem-
ency, and Guido was executed. The court further declared
Pompilia guiltless of the false charge of adultery, and
named her infant son the true-born heir of the Franceschini estates.

This, then, was the framework of Browning's projected
poem. But he did not intend it to be a simple narrative.
Ever since *Pauline,* his first work, one thing fascinated
him: human motivation. In poem after poem he had
searched for the reason behind the act, the half-submerged,
even unconscious forces that propel human nature sometimes against all rational judgment. He knew, too, of the
terrible anguish caused by men who insist upon acting
always in accord with a rigorous set of principles. His own
father-in-law, Edward Moulton Barrett, had been such a

man; he had seen Elizabeth cringe under unbelievable harshness and relentless, unforgiving obduracy. The flight of Pompilia and Caponsacchi may, in a sense, have recalled his own "rescue" of Elizabeth and their "flight" to Italy. Finally, he was aware of the blindness of the law to all but proven fact, and knew instances of the power of the so-called unwritten law, which permitted a self-righteous husband to take revenge. He contemplated the consequences of circumstantial evidence, too, for certainly all appearances were against Pompilia and Caponsacchi, and, in the beginning at least, all sympathy was on Guido's side.

When Browning began actual work on *The Ring and the Book,* he had hoped to finish it within a year. But research, painstaking as always, took time, and there were many interruptions. First he had to attend to the matter of Pen's matriculation at Balliol College, Oxford, which brought about his making the acquaintance of the learned Dr. Benjamin Jowett, rector of the college. The two men were immediately congenial; Jowett wrote of Browning early in 1865,

> I had no idea that there was a perfectly sensible poet in the world, entirely free from enmity, jealousy or other littleness, and thinking no more of himself than if he were an ordinary man.[5]

Through Jowett's friendship and good offices, Browning would be awarded an M.A. by diploma from Oxford in 1867, a seldom-conferred honor which had once been held by Samuel Johnson, whose dictionary Browning had studied so avidly when he had determined on poetry for his career. He was also made honorary fellow of Balliol in 1867, and was offered the professorship of poetry when Matthew Arnold retired. This last honor he declined, though only three lectures a year would have been required of him. He was immersed in the final stages of *The Ring and the Book* by then, and, as he wrote to Isa Blagden, "Three lectures would take as much trouble as three tragedies." [6]

Then, in June, 1866, his father died in Paris after a short illness. Browning had to lay aside *The Ring and the Book* for several months while he settled the estate and brought Sariana back to 19 Warwick Crescent. In November, 1866, there was another interruption, comic rather than tragic. He was summoned to sit on the grand jury of Clerkenwell, where, with his mind filled with the vast canvas of *The Ring and the Book,* he had to take precious time to dutifully listen to the case of a twelve-year-old boy accused of stealing three herrings. The spring of 1867 also found his mind divided; Pen had to go up to Oxford for a preliminary interview with Dr. Jowett. The interview went off well, but Pen's Greek was still not up to Balliol standards, so his father had to engage another tutor for him. Browning's social life was very active, too; he had recently renewed his acquaintance with Annie Egerton-Smith, whom he and Elizabeth had known in Florence. Miss Egerton-Smith was part owner of the Liverpool *Mercury* and very wealthy; she was also devoted to music. Browning, who found in music inspiration as well as joy, was her frequent escort to concerts that season. He dined with Jenny Lind, the "Swedish Nightingale" and paid a call on Anton Rubinstein, the great Russian pianist, who gave him what amounted to a private recital. It was actually with some relief, having visited the Paris Exposition in July, that he went to Brittany in August, where he could settle down to several months of uninterrupted work.

The Ring and the Book, which was published in four separate volumes in November and December, 1868, and January and February, 1869, had grown enormously in concept and scope since the first discovery of "The Old Yellow Book" in 1860. It now included Browning's views on art as well as life; for the binding metaphor which gave the work its title was drawn from his reflection that, just as the alloy in the ring Elizabeth had given him long ago had made possible its creation out of pure gold, so his imagination and poetic craft working on the "gold" of fact had made possible his creation of a poem. He had also thought very deeply about the way in which an individual's point of view can color and change fact, and had decided to present the murder case in twelve dramatic monologues, each spoken by one of the individuals involved, each retelling the same story. (Though there is no evidence of any direct influence, it is interesting to note that Wilkie Collins, the popular writer of mystery novels, had used the same technique in his *The Woman in White,* which had taken London by storm in 1860, in *Armadale* in 1866, and in *The Moonstone,* which was running currently in the magazine *All the Year Round.* No one, however, had yet used it for poetry.) A method which might at first glance seem monotonous became, through Browning's knowledge of human psychology, a brilliant tour de force, in which a jealous husband, a sentimental observer, a judicious rationalist, a wise pope, two lawyers, a priest, a pathetic seventeen-year-old girl, and a crafty villain fighting for his life each gives his own view of the case and his own version of the truth. Each story is identical as to fact; it is the speaker who provides the overtones and also reveals his own character as he speaks. *The Ring and the Book* is Browning's supreme justification of his chosen métier.

Through his various men and women, the poet could give voice to his most deeply felt convictions. Perhaps some of his most startling statements, considering the time in which the book was published, come in Pompilia's monologue, where he permits the dying girl to speak most bluntly about her marriage to a man who hated her, and yet demanded her submission.

> . . . There my husband never used deceit.
> He never did by speech or act imply
> "Because of our soul's yearning that we meet
> And mix in soul through flesh, which yours and mine
> Wear and impress, and make their visible selves,
> —All which means, for the love of you and me,
> Let us become one flesh, being one soul!"
> He only stipulated for the wealth;
> Honest so far. But when he spoke as plain—
> Dreadfully honest also— "Since our souls
> Stand each from each, a whole world's width between,
> Give me the fleshly vesture I can reach
> And rend and leave just fit for hell to burn!"
> Why, in God's name, for Guido's soul's own sake
> Imperilled by polluting mine,—I say,
> I did resist; would I had overcome!

This passage startled the reader of 1868 by its honesty, but there were many who recognized its truth. Pompilia's words strip the veil of hypocrisy from the marriage relationship devoid of love, and they are the more poignant because they are born of instinctive knowledge. She is illiterate and innocent, but she knows better than her judges what true marriage is. Mrs. Sutherland Orr, one of Browning's most devoted friends and his first biographer, saw much of Elizabeth Barrett in Pompilia, especially in her touching concern for her son. Pompilia dies forgiving her murderer, and happy, even, that because of this deed of violence, Guido Franceschini will be prevented from raising the boy to be as evil as himself.

Giuseppe Caponsacchi, the priest, gave Browning the opportunity to explore the rival claims of rule and compassion. According to his vows, Caponsacchi should have "passed by on the other side" and refused to help Pompilia. Up to a point, he obeys these vows, sending cold letters in reply to those which have come to him signed with her name. Then she sends for him. He is a priest. It is his duty to help those who ask. His interest is aroused and he goes to her. To his amazement, she rebukes him for writing of love to her, and he realizes that her husband has forged both his letters and hers in order to trap her. She tells him, as simply as though she were making her confession, of the horror of her life, and implores his help. He wavers, torn between his vows, and the sudden recognition that Christian compassion demands that he help this frightened, distraught, and desperate girl. Before his judges, he asks ironically,

> You understand, of a sudden, gospel, too
> Has a claim here, may possibly pronounce
> Consistent with my priesthood, worthy Christ,
> That I endeavored to save Pompilia?

To their insinuation that he was guilty of Guido's charge, he denies categorically that he had ever loved her "in the way *he* called love!" Through Caponsacchi, Browning voiced his firm belief that love, perfect and complete, can exist between a man and a woman, without physical passion.

> I have done with being judged.
> I stand here guiltless in thought, word and deed,
> To the point that I apprise you,— in contempt
> For all misapprehending ignorance
> O' the human heart, much more the mind of Christ,—
> That I assuredly did bow, was blessed
> By the revelation of Pompilia.

Because he has known and helped Pompilia, he has learned
what being a true priest means:

> . . . see one purpose and one will
> Evolve themselves i' the world, change wrong to right:
> To have to do with nothing but the true,
> The good, the eternal— and these, not alone
> In the main current of the general life,
> But small experiences of every day,
> Concerns of the particular hearth and home:
> To learn not only by a comet's rush
> But a rose's birth,—not by the grandeur, God,—
> But the comfort, Christ.

So Browning expressed his own deep conviction that good
can come out of evil, that from the most sordid situation
something noble and beautiful can rise.

The monologue of the aged pope is the focal point of
the work. In his hands is the power of Guido's life or
death, and Browning made him seem very human as he
ponders the evidence, anxious lest his judgment be wrong.
It is his duty to take into consideration not only fact, but
motive.

> For I am 'ware, it is the seed of act,
> God holds appraising in his hollow palm,
> Not act grown great. . . .

Pompilia and Caponsacchi he immediately acquits of all
culpability, but Guido Franceschini is a more difficult
case. That Guido is guilty of murder is obvious, but, if he
acted in a moment of overwhelming passion, his sentence
might be mitigated. Patiently the pope reviews Guido's
entire life, and finds not one instance wherein cold calcu-
lation did not play a part. Moreover, Guido does not believe that anyone else is capable of a truly disinterested act.

> For I find this black mark impinge the man,—
> That he believes in just the vile of life.

Guido had married Pompilia for her fortune and abused her when he discovered she had none. He had deliberately tried to trap her into making a rendezvous with Caponsacchi, having already accused her of adultery. Most damning of all, he had waited until his son was born and his family succession ensured before murdering her. Guido is evil to the core; cynicism and envy have killed whatever innate compassion he might have possessed. He deserves the ultimate punishment, and not only for murder—this is the least of his crimes. Yet the pope hesitates. It is his obligation as priest and pope to allow a sinner the opportunity to repent. But quickly he realizes that any show of repentance Guido might make would be a lie. Guido has placed himself beyond repentance, and therefore has damned himself. It is not salvation he wants, but physical freedom. The pope decisively signs the execution warrant:

> Enough, for I may die this very night:
> And how should I dare die, this man let live?
> Carry this forthwith to the Governor.

The historical account of the trial given in "The Old Yellow Book" ends with the statement that the pope denied a reprieve, but Browning had not yet finished with the story. He had revealed the mind and heart of goodness in Pompilia, Caponsacchi, and the pope. Now he turned to an equally complete revelation of evil. Guido Franceschini has had his day in court in Book V of *The Ring and the Book*. In a brilliant, sophisticated monologue he has defended his position as a wronged husband defending his honor. But after the pope's verdict, Guido returns in Book XI. He is in prison, awaiting execution. A cardinal and an abbot have come to hear his confession and to give him the last rites. But Guido, facing the gallows, cries out that he is being martyred, that his accusers are liars. He vilifies Pompilia in the most scurrilous language:

> My dowry was derision, my gain—muck,
> My wife (the Church declared my flesh and blood)
> The nameless bastard of a common whore.

He admits defiantly that he hated her, without reason or cause.

> Say that I hated her for no cause
> Beyond my pleasure so to do—what then?

He berates his misfortune that she had lived long enough to testify against him, instead of dying immediately of her wounds as he had intended. He justifies his actions on the ground that he is a *man*, married to a wife "with milk for blood," "a nullity in female shape." He admits that she was good—

> . . . but what's grace
> When you want meat and drink and clothes and fire?

He has hated her goodness, as he has hated all goodness, all his life. Stripped of all pretensions to the nobility he claimed in his defence, he stands revealed as the evil incarnate that the pope has reluctantly judged him.

But it is at the end of his monologue where Browning shows his consummate skill. Guido has proclaimed his unrepentance: "I have lived and died a man and take man's chance." Then he hears footsteps approaching. Suddenly he realizes that the Brotherhood of Death is coming to take him to the gallows. In that instant, all his arrogant bravado dissolves:

Who are these you have let descend my stair?
Ha, their accursed psalm! Lights at the sill!
Is it "Open" they dare bid you? Treachery!
Sirs, have I spoken one word all this while
Out of the world of words I had to say?
Not one word! All was folly—I laughed and mocked!
Sirs, my first true word, all truth and no lie,
Is—save me notwithstanding! Life is all!
I was just stark mad,—let the madman live
Pressed by as many chains as you please pile!
Don't open! Hold me from them! I am yours,
I am the Granduke's—no, I am the Pope's!
Abate,—Cardinal,—Christ,—Maria,—God, . . .
Pompilia, will you let them murder me?

The cringing Guido shrieking frantically the name of his
innocent murdered wife is a stunning reversal of character
and mood which is as overwhelming as it is unexpected.
Browning's artistry creates an unforgettable moment, shattering in its impact. It is not surprising that the concluding section of *The Ring and the Book* becomes a little
pallid beside it. Nothing could surpass Guido's last cry of
agonized despair.

The Ring and the Book was immediately recognized as
Browning's greatest achievement. Reviews were loud in
praise; the *Athenaeum* said it was the "most precious and
profound spiritual treasure that England has produced
since the days of Shakespeare." Neither its length—over
twenty-one thousand lines of blank verse—nor its complex-
ity daunted its readers, though some, like Thomas Carlyle,
were bewildered by it. Carlyle said point-blank that "of all
the strange books produced in this distracted earth by any
of the sons of Adam, this one was altogether the strangest
and most preposterous. . . ."; [7] but the crusty Scot was out-
numbered by those who applauded. The amazing thing
about *The Ring and the Book* is that, despite the method

of having the same story told twelve times, the poem never repeats itself. Each of the speakers in turn throws, as it were, a different spotlight on the central event, and the speaker's mind and point-of-view become as interesting as the story he tells.

Browning rejoiced in the acclaim of *The Ring and the Book*. He was especially pleased that critics noted that he had presented not only individuals, but a whole society, a brilliant pageant of the decadent Rome of the late Renaissance. He also presented an equally brilliant view of humanity itself. For the people of this work do not live only in their own time; they were equally at home in nineteenth-century London, and they remain fully recognizable in our own world. But, most important of all, to the poet and to history, after thirty-five years of effort Browning had proved that his making "men and women speak" was as worthy a vehicle for great poetry as the subjective approach of letting his own soul speak in its own voice. *The Ring and the Book* remains the unsurpassed crown of Browning's work; through it and in it he achieved his own lifelong dream. In December, 1868, he was, at last, a poet—read, recognized, and honored.

10

The honors which came to Robert Browning in the years following the publication of *The Ring and the Book* were a constant surprise to him, even though they gratified him beyond expression. He had never taken a college degree, yet he was offered the rectorship of two universities—St. Andrews and the University of Glasgow—not once, but twice, by unanimous vote of students and faculty. The St. Andrews offer must especially have pleased him, for that office had formerly been held by John Stuart Mill, whose criticism of *Pauline* had forced him to break new ground in poetry and to find his own creative medium. Oxford had already granted him an honorary degree; in 1879, he was awarded a Doctor of Letters by Cambridge, and in 1882, Oxford conferred upon him a Doctor of Civil Laws. The University of Edinburgh also gave him an honorary degree, and the tumultuous reception that the students there accorded him prompted him to make his first and last impromptu speech.

The degree he accepted with humility and gratitude; the rectorships he declined. He had no taste for administrative work, and, besides, he was fully occupied with his poetry. Between the publication of Volume IV of *The Ring and the Book* in 1869 and his death twenty years later, he published fifteen volumes of completely new work. Much of his later poetry has fallen into undeserved oblivion, and even in his own lifetime it was overshadowed by the titanic *The Ring and the Book*. But Browning was not one to rest on his laurels, and he did not hesitate to experiment with new ideas, even to basing a long poem,

Red Cotton Night-cap Country, on contemporary events and thereby risking the possibility of a lawsuit.

He certainly enjoyed all the additional benefits of being a celebrity. He sat for portraits, marble busts, and photographs. His letters provide fascinating glimpses of his social life: he lunches with Prince and Princess Christian (Queen Victoria's daughter, Helena, and son-in-law) at Lady Stanley's, and meets Disraeli at a dinner party. He spends a Christmas holiday at Hatfield House, country seat of the third Marquess of Salisbury, and meets the shah of Persia at a "gentlemen only" banquet. He notes the enthusiastic reception accorded a new symphony of Johannes Brahms under the baton of the celebrated violinist-conductor Joseph Joachim, and remarks on Joachim's superb rendition of the Beethoven violin concerto at the same concert. Later he goes to Cambridge to see Joachim invested with the honorary degree of Doctor of Music. With Miss Egerton-Smith he attends the newly established "Pop" Concerts, hearing Clara Schumann and Anton Rubinstein, and enjoying soirees in their honor afterwards. He goes to art exhibits and to the theatre. He sees a new young actor named Henry Irving dazzle all London in a second-rate play called *The Bells* in 1871. Ten years later he is in the audience on the opening night of Tennyson's new play, *The Cup,* starring that same Henry Irving and a sensational young actress named Ellen Terry. He dines with Joseph Jefferson, the American actor, who is playing a London engagement in *Rip Van Winkle,* and he courteously arranges for the visiting Italian actor, Tommaso Salvini, to have guest privileges at the Athenaeum Club.

Nor were his literary colleagues neglected. The old names—Carlyle, Dickens, Rossetti, and Tennyson constantly recur in his correspondence; but new ones are added: Swinburne, who receives a gracious letter thanking him for a perceptive critique; Matthew Arnold, who is urged to restore *Empedocles on Etna* to his collected works; Edward FitzGerald, poet of the *Rubaiyat;* Edmund Gosse, the literary historian and critic; Francis Palgrave, compiler of *The Golden Treasury;* Sir George Grove, musicologist and editor of *Dictionary of Music and Musicians.* To say nothing of that thorn in his flesh, Alfred Austin, whose poetry Browning thought worse than second rate, and whose savage criticism of successive Browning volumes finally led him to strike back in 1876, in a poem called "Of Pacchiarotto and How He Worked in Distemper." In 1879, he accepted the presidency of the new Shakespeare Society; and 1881 brought the honor that bewildered him even as he rejoiced in it—the formation of the Browning Society by two hundred interested individuals, *none* of whom was a personal friend. No other living poet had been so recognized. Browning received this accolade with amusement, sincerely unbelieving that anyone could really be sufficiently interested in his work to want to study it. But an American Browning Society was formed shortly thereafter, and soon every sizable city in England and the United States boasted a local chapter. Browning frequently found himself wavering between pleasure and wry amusement, for the efforts of society members to explain his poetry frequently engendered more heat than light. There is a story, which may not be apocryphal, of his attending a meeting of the London Society, sitting in the back of the room where his presence would not be quickly remarked, and listening to a zealous member put all kinds of erroneous interpretations into a particular poem. Finally, unable to listen any longer, Browning interrupted to explain what he *had* meant, only to be assured by the membership in chorus that he was quite wrong!

On the face of it, his life now seemed one of profitable

work and the enjoyment of well-earned rewards. Beneath that surface, however, all was not quite so serene. The immediately favorable reception of Volume I of *The Ring and the Book* in November, 1868, was dulled for him because Pen had failed his entrance examinations for Balliol. Pen did manage to matriculate at Christ Church College, Oxford, in January, 1869; but Browning had set his heart on Balliol for his son and was deeply disappointed. His disappointment increased when he discovered that Pen was not measuring up to university standards. It was at this point that the distressing episode occurred which brought with it the nearest approach to scandal ever to enter Browning's life.

In the summer of 1869, he took Pen and Sariana on a tour of Scotland. August found them at the home of Lady Louisa Ashburton at Loch Luichert. Browning was now fifty-seven, no longer the dashing young dandy who had amused his friends in the 1830's by his fancy waistcoats and lemon-yellow kid gloves. He was now a distinguished poet, in the prime of life, with a vigor and enthusiasm which made him seem at least ten years younger. As was inevitable, there had been some speculation as to whether he would ever marry again, and his name had already been linked with that of Jean Ingelow, best remembered now for her children's stories, whose volume of poems had received critical approval in 1863. Browning had laughingly denied that particular matrimonial possibility, saying that he had only the slightest acquaintance with the lady and that her astonishment at the rumor probably exceeded his. Actually the idea of a second marriage seemed almost sacrilegious to him. But in August, 1869, he was deeply depressed about his son. He felt that perhaps he had been mistaken in trying to raise the boy by himself. There were many ways in which a mother's influence was more effective than a father's, and Pen had been denied this. Socially, too, a wife could be of help to him; Sariana was a devoted sister, but she cared very little for dinner parties and balls, and 19 Warwick Crescent was perhaps too staid and quiet for a young man who liked the gaiety and excitement he found in his friends' homes. For the first time, Browning gave serious thought to a second marriage, and at this crucial moment he was the house guest of one of the most beautiful, witty, and wealthy ladies he had ever known.

Louisa Mackenzie, Lady Ashburton, has been variously described as a designing woman intent on catching a second wealthy husband, and as the grievously injured victim of Browning's cruelty. Both portraits are equally incorrect. As heiress of the vast Mackenzie estates she would have been independently wealthy even without the fortune her husband had left her, and there is ample evidence that she had suitors of rank and fortune to spare. She was certainly a strikingly handsome woman—tall, graceful and regal, with black hair and flashing black eyes, and a well modulated voice that was one of her greatest charms. She was also extremely intelligent. She was known to her friends as a warm-hearted, impulsive person, quick-tempered, but generous. That she was attracted by Robert Browning was obvious, but there is not the slightest evidence that she in any way pursued him.

Browning was equally attracted by her. He had met her at a dinner party in London, and found her both sympathetic and charming. That he should be her guest at Loch Luichert at the conclusion of his Scottish tour was a natural outcome of their almost immediate friendship. He found her stimulating, even exciting, and he knew that a marriage to her would be regarded as eminently suitable. She was a superb hostess, a good companion, and she seemed to be quite amenable to the idea of taking on Pen. She was not, of course, remotely like Elizabeth Barrett, and she could not in any way affect Browning's loyalty and devotion to his wife's memory. There could be only one Elizabeth Barrett. But his regard for Lady Ashburton was sufficiently great to make him feel that he could honorably offer her marriage.

Apparently he proposed to her in September, 1869, but he frankly told her that his heart was buried in Florence, and that he was considering a second marriage mainly because of the possible benefit to his son. Lady Ashburton furiously declined his proposal, and told all her friends how brutally she had been treated. Since many of her friends were also Browning's, there was the inevitable taking of sides and considerable gossip. Browning returned to London, grieved at having been the cause of such unpleasantness, but it is possible that he was actually relieved at her rejection of him. Pen's continued failure at Oxford did nothing to raise his spirits, and when the young man was "sent down"—i.e., flunked out—in the spring of 1870, Browning wrote to George Barrett and Isa Blagden that he felt as though his entire life had been wasted. He spent the summer of 1870 in Brittany, but the respite he might have gained from that holiday was little; the Franco-Prussian War was raging, and he had to leave hurriedly early in September because there were rumors that he was to be arrested as a German spy! He returned to London, feeling decidedly at odds with the world, and spent the winter working on *Balaustion's Adventure,* a poem set in classical Greece and based on his knowledge of Euripides, and the wickedly satiric poem about Louis Napoleon entitled *Prince Hohenstiel-Schwangau, Saviour of Society.* Both were published late in 1871.

During the spring of 1871, he was surprised to receive

several notes from Lady Ashburton, the last of which invited him to pay another visit to Loch Luichert. He was not minded to do a repeat performance as a house guest, but he had been planning a Scottish holiday; so, in August, 1871, he arranged to drive over for a short call. He hoped to mend a broken friendship which he had valued, and Lady Ashburton's notes had given him the firm impression that she had the same thought in mind. But he was quickly shown that this was not the case at all. Lady Ashburton, as he wrote later to Edith Storey (daughter of William Wetmore Storey, the sculptor whom he had known at Florence), wanted only "to have the air of shutting the door in my face," [1] and had invited him for the sole purpose of telling him that his proposal of marriage had been most unwelcome. Browning, stung to the quick, was embarrassed and annoyed, and from what can be pieced together from very scanty evidence, Lady Ashburton provoked an unpleasant quarrel which she did not hesitate to describe to all her friends. They, in turn, added to its proportions until a violent storm of gossip was created, leaving Browning exhausted and heartily disliking Lady Ashburton for having disclosed what should have remained private.

The letters he wrote to a very few close personal friends early in 1872 are most reticent; only initials are used, but their tone of disgust and self-castigation over the "detestable subject" comes through clearly. Fourteen years later in 1886, he could view "the calumnies which Lady A. exploded in all the madness of her wounded vanity" [2] more objectively. But in 1872 he found the entire episode repellent in the extreme. His repugnance, compounded by the humiliation he felt for having contributed unwittingly to the desecration of Elizabeth's memory, accounts for the sardonic mood of *Fifine at the Fair*, which he began shortly after that visit to Scotland and had ready for publication in May, 1872. *Fifine at the Fair,* with its sophisticated, cynical hero Don Juan, who wavers between his loyalty to his devoted wife and his overwhelming physical attraction for Fifine the gypsy girl—and gives logical reasons for preferring Fifine's attractions, at least for the moment—bewildered and perplexed the Browning Society, because it seemed such a departure from their poet's usual firm stand on moral values. The few people who recognized the source of self-flagellation in it remained discreetly silent, however, and gradually the Lady Ashburton affair passed into oblivion. But its effect on Browning was to be a lasting one. It brought a darker cast to his poetry, which became more soul-searching and less exuberant after this experience.

Meanwhile, there was still the problem of Pen's education. Browning was reconciled to the fact that his son would never be a scholar; he wrote Isa Blagden, "I am relieved about Pen by knowing the very worst of the poor boy." [3] Nevertheless, it was unthinkable that Pen should be permitted to drift without any purpose. Browning consulted George Barrett, who was now a prominent attorney, about the possibility of Pen's studying law, but that seemed inadvisable. The only thing Pen really liked and seemed to have some talent for was painting, and Browning gradually came to the conclusion that his son might possibly become an artist. Through Rossetti, he had met the painter John Everett Millais, and he asked Millais for an opinion. Millais, after a "viewing," said that Pen actually had considerable talent, and should be encouraged to study.

So, in 1874, Pen was sent to Antwerp to study with Jean Arnould Heyermans, the teacher Millais had recommended, where he made excellent progress. By 1878, Browning was arranging a showing of his son's work in

London, assuring the aged Thomas Carlyle that, if he would honor the occasion, he would find the exhibit placed so that he need climb no stairs. The following year Pen had another one-man show, and in 1880 one of his pictures achieved the coveted honor of being exhibited at the Hanover Gallery. He also took up sculpture, and one of his statues, "The Dryope," received an honorable mention at the Paris Salon. Browning's anxiety changed to delight and pride at his son's success, even though it meant that they were separated from each other much of the time. But to this he was reconciled. Pen had never outgrown his early upbringing in Italy; he had never become a proper English boy. He had always found the Continent more congenial, and certainly there was more there to see and to paint than in England, so Browning let him go with his blessing, even as his own father had done for him.

With Pen's future work assured, Browning's life settled into a comfortable routine. From November until the end of July he was in London, and each summer he and Sariana took a leisurely holiday on the Continent, to give him an opportunity to work uninterruptedly at his newest book. Between 1873 and 1880 he published eight volumes, an astonishing output for a man in his sixties. They show an equally astonishing variety of subject matter and theme. *Red Cotton Night-cap Country* (1873) was based on the suicide of a mentally deranged young man in Normandy in 1870; his last will and testament was being argued in the courts at the very moment that Browning was writing the poem. One of the principles involved in the case, the young man's mistress, even permitted the poet to interview her, thus giving him a closer and infinitely more realistic view than that presented to the judge or the jury. But Browning did not use the dramatic monologue approach for this work; instead he used the straight narrative form he had tried in *Sordello*—and *Red Cotton Night-cap Country* was disliked as heartily as was *Sordello*. Robert Browning was not a poet Wilkie Collins. *Aristophanes' Apology* (1875), a sequel to *Balaustion's Adventure,* which drew on Browning's deep knowledge of the classic Greek dramatists for its subject matter, fared better, though it was admired more for its erudition than for its poetry. *The Inn Album* (also 1875) was based on his interest in a celebrated libel case of the 1830's. Of *Pacchiarotto and How He Worked in Distemper, with Other Poems* (1876) was a collection of short pieces which was fairly well received. The year 1877 brought Browning's long-awaited translation of the *Agammenon* of Aeschylus, which he had undertaken at the behest of Thomas Carlyle. Carlyle, however, did not like the translation at all, nor did Browning when he had finished with it; indeed, he was rather dubious thereafter about Matthew Arnold's enthusiasm for Greek literature.

The years had brought sadness to him as well as success. Charles Dickens had died in 1870, and Isa Blagden in 1872, both good friends, and Browning felt their losses keenly. Then, in September, 1877, Annie Egerton-Smith died suddenly at La Saisiaz in the Swiss Alps, where she had gone to join Browning and his sister for their holiday. Browning was profoundly shocked and saddened by this tragedy, and he spent the winter writing a long poem, *La Saisiaz,* as a memorial tribute to her. In it he considered the entire question of the soul's immortality, concluding once again, as he had in *Christmas Eve and Easter Day,* that human knowledge can prove nothing about eternity, and that man must rely on the intuition of his heart for faith that Love exists in eternity beyond this earth as well as in time and space. The Victorian is often disliked and derided for what is termed his preoccupation with death. But such derision fails to take into account the temper of the age. The Victorians for the most part, believed not only in law and order, but also in proper preparation for the next event. Their contemplation of death as life's last great event in this world was not a result of morbidity for its own sake, but rather based on the firm conviction that one's eternity would be determined by the preparation one had made for it on earth. As Browning wrote in *La Saisiaz,*

> I have lived, then, done and suffered, loved and hated,
> learnt and taught
> This—there is no reconciling wisdom with a world dis-
> traught,
> Goodness with triumphant evil, power with failure in
> the aim,
> If—(to my own sense, remember! though none other
> feel the same!)
> If you bar me from assuming earth to be a pupil's place,
> And life, time—with their chances, changes— just pro-
> bation-space,
> Mine, for me.

The same conviction which had led him to write on the fly-leaf of Elizabeth's Bible in 1861, "Thus I believe, thus I affirm, thus I am certain it is, that from this life I shall pass to another, there, where that lady lives of whom my soul was enamoured," led to his triumphant cry in *La Saisiaz,*

> I affirm and reaffirm it therefore: only make as plain
> As that man now lives, that, after dying, man will live
> again—
> Make as plain the absence, also, of a law to contravene
> Voluntary passage from this life to that by change of
> scene,—
> And I bid him—at suspicion of first cloud athwart his
> sky,
> Flower's departure, forest's arrival—never hesitate, but
> die!

Readers of *La Saisiaz* in 1878 liked the poem, and found in it much the same comfort that Tennyson had given them in *In Memoriam,* a quarter of a century earlier. It is seldom read today, except for its prologue, which is deservedly remembered as one of Robert Browning's most beautifully eloquent statements:

> Good, to forgive;
>   Best, to forget!
>   Living, we fret;
> Dying, we live.
> Fretless and free,
>   Soul, clap thy pinion!
>   Earth have dominion,
> Body, o'er thee!

11

In August, 1878, Browning suddenly decided that he wanted to visit Italy again. He did not want to go to Brittany or Switzerland; the memory of Annie Egerton-Smith was too poignantly connected with both those places, but he did want to get out of England for a time, and it had been seventeen years since he had basked in the Italian sun. He would not go to Florence; that he could not bring himself to contemplate. But he did want to see Asolo and Venice. With Sariana for a companion, he crossed the Channel, took the new railroad as far into southern France as it went, then proceeded by carriage and muleback to Splügen Pass. Here he remained for several weeks. He found the mountain scenery exhilarating, and he was able to work concentratedly at his new volume, *Dramatic Idyls I*. In fact, he worked for so many hours at a stretch that Sariana told him sternly that they would have to leave, and go somewhere where there would be greater intrusion on his time, if he did not observe a more reasonable pace. He saw the sense of this good humoredly, and made several intrusions on his time himself.

In September, however, they were at Asolo, with Browning excitedly reliving everything he had experienced on his first visit there, forty years before. He shouted from the top of the ruined castle and the echo returned, just as he had remembered it. The old inn was gone, but the primitive hospitality of the new one was just as satisfactory, if not more so. And Venice was just as fantastically beautiful as his memory had cherished it. He decided, then and there, that Venice would be the place for all his future holidays; and, except for one year when Sariana was too weak from a peritonitis attack to take a long journey and they vacationed in Wales instead, every autumn thereafter was spent in the city of the gondolas, where Browning hobnobbed with the Spanish royal family and other visiting elite.

Dramatic Idyls I occupied him during the winter of 1878, and was published in April, 1879. It was an immediate success, mainly because it was not as philosophical or psychological as his other works. The six long poems were stories first and character delineations afterwards, and not one could be called obscure. "Pheidippides," the story of the runner who brought the news of the victory at Marathon, and "Ivan Ivanovitch," a grisly Russian folk tale, were especially enjoyed and admired. Browning followed this collection in 1880 with *Dramatic Idyls II,* which, though not as successful as *Dramatic Idyls I,* nevertheless had a most satisfactory reception.

The years passed swiftly. On his seventieth birthday, in 1882, the Browning Societies of England and America honored the poet by a gift of a set of his complete works bound in green morocco, in a carved oak velvet-lined case. Browning was thrilled by that "wonderful Book case and Books" that, as he put it, "glorified" [1] his birthday. This was also the year when Oxford conferred the Doctor of Civil Laws upon him, and, to his delight, a waggish undergraduate in the gallery dangled a red-cotton nightcap above his head. This intrusion into such solemnity might have brought stern punishment to the culprit, but Browning enjoyed the joke hugely, and his intercession forestalled official administrative wrath.

Jocoseria, another volume of short poems, "gravish and gayish" as he described them, was published in the spring of 1883. He considered the book a trifle, but it had amazing success; and one poem, "Never the Time and the Place," showed that he had not lost his skill as a lyricist.

> Never the time and the place
>   And the loved one all together!
> This path—how soft to pace!
>   This May—what magic weather!
> Where is the loved one's face?
> In a dream that the loved one's face meets mine,
>   But the house is narrow, the place is bleak
> Where, outside, rain and wind combine
>   With a furtive ear, if I strive to speak,
>   With a hostile eye at my flushing cheek,
> With a malice that marks each word, each sign!
> O enemy sly and serpentine,
>   Uncoil thee from the waking man!
>   Do I hold the Past
>   Thus firm and fast
> Yet doubt if the Future hold I can?
> This path so soft to pace shall lead
> Through the magic of May to herself indeed!
> Or narrow if needs the house must be,
> Outside are the storms and strangers: we—
> Oh, close, safe, warm sleep I and she,
>   —I and she!

He had written no more exquisite love poetry during the period when he courted Elizabeth Barrett.

His next book, however, was a complete change of pace. The idea for *Ferishtah's Fancies*, published in November, 1884, was drawn from his memory of a book of Oriental fables which he had read as a boy, but his fables were all his own invention, and so was Ferishtah, the wise Moslem sage, who teaches that man must not desert mankind to enjoy a selfish solitude, even to advance his own creative and spiritual gifts. The poem also, once again, voices Browning's conviction that human relations must ultimately depend on mutual trust and love, especially in those areas where reason and intellect are inoperative. Some critics have presented *Ferishtah's Fancies* as evidence of Browning's essential anti-intellectuality, but nothing could be further from the truth. Long ago, in *Paracelsus*, in the character of Aprile, he had expressed his disapproval of ungoverned emotionalism. But, in an age becoming more and more rationalistic, he just as vigorously warned against too much reasoning and too many blueprints. His own time supplied him with enough cause for such a warning; General Gordon had been under siege at Khartoum in the Sudan for months, pleading for troops and supplies to stave off what would certainly become a massacre at the hands of the Fuzzy-Wuzzies, and official London had argued and reasoned and discussed. The relief column had been dispatched a bare eight weeks before *Ferishtah's Fancies* was published, too late to save Gordon. Life, Browning insisted, cannot depend completely on long-drawn-out conclusions, however sincere the motives. There are too many intangibles and imponderables which must be met with swift comprehension and decision, if they are to be met at all.

The next three years were spent at work upon the volume which Robert Browning hoped would be the final, definitive statement of his philosophy. Ever since *The Ring and the Book,* he had been deluged with requests for his autobiography, or for permission to have his biography written. He had unequivocally refused all these requests and for a number of years had been systematically destroying all his private papers, except for the letters he and Elizabeth had written to each other, lest they fall into unsympathetic hands. Froude's biography of Carlyle, published in 1882, had infuriated him by its bias and he was determined not to suffer the same fate. He was, however, eager to make his philosophical position as clear as possible. *Parleyings with Certain People of Importance in Their Day*, published in 1887, was the culmination of all his life's experience and observation. Art, poetry, music, politics, and religion—all came under his scrutiny for the last time. His method was to call up out of the past a notable personage in each of these fields and represent himself as in discussion with him. The persons he chose were those he had learned to know and love in the books he had read in his father's library when he was a boy. They were relatively unknown to readers of 1887, however, and thus the book was almost unintelligible to critics of the time; though some did recognize the attack on Carlyle's pessimism (with which Browning, despite his friendship for Carlyle personally, had never agreed) in the "Parleying with Bernard de Mandeville," and the cleverly satiric portrait of Disraeli in the "Parleying with George Bubb Dodington." To those who have followed the growth of Browning's convictions, these "final statements" come as no surprise. They merely reinforce and express more fully what he had always believed.

The lack of critical approval for *Parleyings* did not perturb Robert Browning. He had long since learned to discount critical opinion and to wait, confidently, for his books eventually to find their audience. And there was so much excitement in his own family that everything else paled by comparison. Pen had become engaged. The lady was Fannie Coddington, an American, whom he had met in London when she had visited there in 1872. He had proposed to her at that time—unbeknownst to his father—and had been rejected. But they had renewed their acquaintance during Fannie's second visit to England in 1886, and Pen, who had never stopped loving her, proposed again, and this time was accepted. Browning was amazed by this evidence of his son's unsuspected tenacity and delighted by his choice.

> Now it happens, of all the young persons of my
> acquaintance, I could not pick out a single one so
> fitted—if I am any judge at all,—to make Pen, with
> his many peculiarities, the best of wives.[2]

he wrote to friends, telling them of the engagement. Fannie, many years later, recalled how he had greeted her at their first meeting after Pen's announcement: "I have always wanted a daughter and now I have one!" [3] and that he never once used the term "daughter-in-law" when he spoke of her. The young couple were married in London in October, honeymooned in Italy, and then went to New York so that Fannie might make the necessary arrangements for becoming a European resident. Browning hoped that they would make their home in London, but when they decided on Venice, he made no objection and bought the enormous Palazzo Rezonicco for them as his wedding gift. He spent three months with them in Venice during the summer of 1888, and enjoyed himself hugely helping Pen and Fannie to restore and furnish their new home.

His health in the past two years had not been good. He had caught numerous colds and suffered recurrences of what his doctor called "spasmodic asthma." But, since he was quite unconcerned about his physical condition, even Sariana was not unduly anxious. During the winter of 1888–89 he was, as usual, at work on another volume of poems, and also undertaking the Herculean task of revising and re-editing his collected works. He continued his round of dinner parties and visits; his engagement book was filled for weeks in advance. In June, 1889, he went up to Cambridge, and spent a Sunday with the Fellows of Trinity College. Edmund Gosse, in his *Personalia,* recalled vividly that afternoon, with Browning in the best of spirits reminiscing about his youth, marveling, "as he looked back, at the audacious obstinacy which had made him, when a youth, determine to be a poet and nothing but a poet." He held the group spellbound with a story he had heard in Tuscany forty years earlier, and then went on to show how he could make a poem of it. Only a few of those present noticed that he looked rather frail.

In September, 1889, he set out for his annual Italian pilgrimage. Sariana, of course, accompanied him. They stopped at Asolo; it was unseasonably cold, but Browning insisted on taking his usual long walks, though he found that breathing was sometimes very difficult for him. He fell in love with a ruined tower, and promptly decided to buy it. He would rebuild it as a summer retreat, he said, and christen it "Pippa's Tower." He put the negotiations in the hands of a local agent; then he and Sariana left for Venice.

Pen made great progress with the Palazzo Rezonicco even to putting in a furance. Browning inspected the house from attic to ground floor and was loud in his praise. The weather was warm, perfect for gondola rides and walks in the Lido. Additional excitement was provided by the arrival of the proofs of his new book, *Asolando*. On a Sunday afternoon he read some of the poems aloud to Fannie. When he came to the "Epilogue," he read the first two stanzas, then paused. "Now, what I have said here may sound conceited, but I believe it is true," he remarked. "And, as it's true, it shall stand." [4] Then he read the third stanza:

> One who never turned his back but marched breast forward,
>   Never doubted clouds would break,
> Never dreamed, though right were worsted, wrong would triumph,
> Hold we fall to rise, are baffled to fight better,
>   Sleep to wake.

It was the summation of his life's creed.

But it was autumn, even in Venice, and in late November fog turned the weather dank and cold. Browning insisted, nevertheless, on his daily walks, and came home from one of them with a chill. The cold settled on his chest, causing violent paroxysms of coughing, but he would not hear of calling a doctor, even when asthma made it almost impossible for him to breathe. There was too much to do! Pen and Fannie had taken a box at the opera for *Carmen,* which he had always wanted to hear, for he had met the author of the original *Carmen,* Prosper Mérimée, in Paris, in 1855. He enjoyed the performance thoroughly, but when he returned home, he could hardly climb the stairs to his room. The next morning he reluctantly agreed to seeing a doctor, but he stubbornly refused to stay in bed. He was on his feet and fully dressed when the doctor arrived. The doctor prescribed bed rest immediately, and linseed poultices for his chest, and—with utmost gravity —frequent doses of digitalis. The heart had been affected, but no one could say how much. Browning repeatedly said that he was suffering no pain. He was able to examine the advance copy of *Asolando* and was pleased to find no errors in it. Not until the afternoon of December 12 did he suddenly whisper to his son, "I feel much worse. I know now that I must die."

His mind wandered intermittently all that evening. Sariana remained at his beside, holding back her tears, talking with him quietly, helping him to remember things he felt troubled at forgetting. Fannie and Pen were nearby in an adjoining room. A telegram arrived from London, saying that the entire first edition of *Asolando* had sold out on that same day. He was told this good news and understood; he smiled and murmured, "Very gratifying." Two hours later, as the bells of San Marco chimed ten, he died. On the ceiling over his head, the picture his son had painted, inspired by a passage from Shelley's *The Revolt of Islam,* faded into shadows cast by dimmed lamps.

ଊଊଊଊଊଊଊଊଊଊଊଊ ଊଊଊଊଊଊଊଊଊଊଊଊଊଊଊଊଊ ଊଊଊଊଊଊଊଊଊ

The beautiful Church of England services were recited in the grand sala of the Palazzo Rezonicco on September 16. Telegraphed messages of sympathy from Queen Victoria and King Victor Emanuel of Italy were read, and all the officials of Venice attended. The municipality sent the Golden Barge, with the angel at the prow and the lion at the stern, and a company of *pompieri* in dress uniforms to bring Robert Browning to San Michele, the cemetery island. The Golden Barge was followed by a procession of black gondolas, as the city mourned the poet who had so loved Italy and had written of it so magnificently. The casket, covered with a purple pall and surrounded by flowers, was guarded by the *pompieri* while it waited in state at the private chapel on San Michele until arrangements were completed to bring it to England. It had been decided that Robert Browning must receive that final honor due to greatness—burial in Westminster Abbey.

The services were held on the last day of the year. London had been gripped by a thick yellow fog; but, just as the cortege arrived at the Abbey, the sun broke through, streaming across the huge congregation, all in black, who rose as one when the casket was carried through the nave into the choir. All who witnessed the funeral were struck by the fact that the people there were not just interested, or even curious observers; one and all had come to do homage. The number of young people present was remarkable. Hallam Tennyson acted as an honorary pallbearer, and the poet laureate's wreath of violets and roses lay on the pall. Representatives from Oxford, Cambridge, and the University of Edinburgh also marched in the procession. The Queen had sent Captain Walter Campbell as her personal representative; the French and Italian ministers of state and the American ambassador were also in attendance. This, on the day before the biggest, most important holiday of the year! The entire service was chanted by the Abbey choir and had been composed especially for the occasion by Sir Frederick Bridge. The anthem was a choral setting of Elizabeth Barrett Browning's poem "The Sleep," and, before the benediction, the entire congregation was asked to join in singing "Our God, Our Help in Ages Past." Then, to music as solemn and splendid as any that Abt Vogler could have composed, the procession moved reverently into the Poet's Corner for the burial. Childe Roland's pilgrimage was over, but the Dark Tower was dark no longer. It was filled with the sound of music and ablaze with light.

꧁꧁꧁꧁꧁꧁꧁꧁꧁꧁꧁꧁꧁꧁꧁꧁꧁꧁꧁꧁꧁꧁꧁꧁꧁꧁꧁꧁꧁

On the night of May 7, 1812, a great comet had flared across the sky. The year after Browning's death, William Sharp, his first biographer, said that on December 12, 1889, a new star had been discovered in the constellation of Orion the Hunter. Though this statement has since been proven false (the result of an amateur astronomer's error), it perhaps represents that kind of national wishful thinking which from time immemorial has promulgated myths about great men. Certainly the English people had shown, by their homage at the Abbey, their recognition that a "star" had vanished from their immediate midst, and its seeming reappearance in the heavens is consonant with the traditionally classic bent of the Victorian mind.

For the twentieth century, however, the new star—which, incidentally, would probably have regaled Robert Browning considerably—is an unnecessary, rather incongruous embellishment. If we must speculate, it is more likely that on the night of December 12, 1889, ". . . the stars of night beat with emotion," to quote the moving lines from "Saul" —that

> There were witnesses, cohorts about me, to left and to right,
> Angels, powers, the unuttered, unseen, the alive, the aware.

A man who had taken a blazing comet as prophetic of his own future, who had called upon men of all time everywhere to "greet the unseen with a cheer," who viewed death as "one fight more,/The best and the last!", would not anticipate a passive eternity. But even such speculation is unnecessary, and irrelevant. For life was what mattered to Robert Browning, "intensest life," lived completely, to the uttermost, wholly committed and involved, conquering all obstacles and meeting all hazards with a vital faith in creation's essential goodness—forever in joy!

> All that I know
>   Of a certain star
> Is, it can throw
>   (Like an angled spar)
> Now a dart of red,
>   Now a dart of blue;
> Till my friends have said
>   They would fain see, too,
> My star that dartles the red and the blue!
> Then it stops like a bird; like a flower hangs furled:
>   They must solace themselves with Saturn above it.
> What matter to me if their star is a world?
>   Mine has opened its soul to me; and therefore
>   I love it.

NOTES

Chapter 1
1. Hood, 93.
2. *Letters,* II, 474.

Chapter 2
1. *Pauline.*
2. Griffin & Minchin, 59.

Chapter 3
1. Macready, *Diaries,* December 7, 1835.
2. *Ibid.,* December 31.
3. Griffiin & Minchin, 105.
4. *New Letters,* 12.
5. Macready, August 3, 1836.
6. *Ibid.,* March 29.
7. *Ibid.,* April 18.
8. Harriet Martineau, *Autobiography,* ed. Chapman (Boston, 1877), II, 325
9. Hood, 2.
10. *Ibid.,* 3.
11. Griffin & Minchin, 90.
12. Macready, September 5, 1839.
13. T. R. Lounsbury, *The Early Literary Career of Robert Browning* (New York: Scribner's, 1911), 92.

Chapter 4
1. *Poems,* 128.
2. *Letters,* I, 28.
3. *Browning and Domett,* 36.

4. *New Letters*, 25.
5. *Ibid.*
6. *Ibid.*, 29.
7. See, John Forster, *Life of Dickens* (1873), II, 25.
8. *Browning and Domett*, 63-64.
9. Griffin & Minchin, 119.
10. *Ibid.*

Chapter 5
1. Griffin & Minchin, 148.
2. *Letters*, I, 2-3.
3. *Ibid.*, 6.
4. *Ibid.*, 26.
5. *Ibid.*, 41.
6. *Ibid.*, 60.
7. Taplin, 152.
8. *Letters*, II, 335.
9. *Ibid.*, I, 176–7.
10. *Ibid.*, 178.
11. *Ibid.*, 285.
12. *Ibid.*, 302.
13. *Ibid.*, 310.
14. *Ibid.*, 253.
15. *Ibid.*, 407.
16. *Ibid.*, 437.
17. *Ibid.*, II, 270.
18. *Ibid.*, 537.
19. *Twenty-Two Unpublished Letters*, 3.
20. *Ibid.*
21. *Letters*, II, 544.
22. *Ibid.*, 547.
23. *Ibid.*, 567.

Chapter 6
1. Taplin, 182.
2. *Twenty-Two Unpublished Letters*, 2.
3. *Ibid.*, 16.

4. *Ibid.*

5. Orr, 147.

6. Griffin & Minchin, 162.

7. *Twenty-Two Unpublished Letters,* 57-58.

8. *Letters of E.B.B.,* I, 383.

9. *Twenty-Two Unpublished Letters,* 60.

10. *Ibid.,* 63.

11. *Ibid.,* 68-9.

Chapter 7

1. See, *Letters of Charles Eliot Norton,* ed. Sara Norton & M. Q. DeWolfe Howe (Boston & New York, 1913), I, 79.

2. Orr, 164.

3. Griffin & Minchin, 189.

4. Orr, 191.

Chapter 8

1. See, Nathaniel Hawthorne, *Passages from French and Italian Notebooks* (Boston and New York: Houghton Mifflin, 1913, Vol. X of Riverside Edn.), 336.

2. Griffin and Minchin, 218.

3. Hood, 62.

Chapter 9

1. *Isa,* 82.

2. *Ibid.,* 92.

3. *Ibid.,* 104.

4. *Ibid.,* 193.

5. Griffin & Minchin, 232.

6. *Isa,* 254.

7. See D. A. Wilson, and D. W. Macarthur, *Carlyle in Old Age* (1865-1881), New York, E. P. Dutton, 1934, 136.

Chapter 10

1. Hood, 326.

2. *Ibid.,* 336.

3. *Isa,* 364.

Chapter 11

1. *New Letters,* 274.

2. Hood, 274.

3. Fannie Barrett Browning, *Some Memories of Robert Browning,* 10.

4. *Poems,* 1007.

BIBLIOGRAPHY

Main Sources

The Letters of Robert Browning and Elizabeth Barrett Browning, two vols. in one, London, John Murray, 1934. *(Letters)*

Twenty-Two Unpublished Letters of Elizabeth Barrett Browning and Robert Browning, Addressed to Henrietta and Arabella Moulton Barrett, Peekskill, Crosbie Gaige's Watch Hill Press, 1935.

Letters of Robert Browning Collected by T. J. Wise, Ed. Thurman L. Hood, New Haven, Yale University Press, 1933. (Hood)

New Letters of Robert Browning, Ed. William Clyde DeVane and Kenneth Leslie Knickerbocker, New Haven, Yale University Press, 1950. *(New Letters)*

Letters of the Brownings to George Barrett, Ed. Paul Landis, Urbana, University of Illinois Press, 1958.

Dearest Isa: Robert Browning's Letters to Isabella Blagden, Ed. Edward C. McAleer, Austin, University of Texas Press, 1951. *(Isa)*

Robert Browning and Alfred Domett, Frederic G. Kenyon, editor, London, Smith, Elder, 1906.

Robert Browning and Julia Wedgwood: A Broken Friendship as Revealed by Their Letters, Ed. Richard Curle, London, Murray and Cape, 1937.

The Letters of Elizabeth Barrett Browning, Ed. Frederic G. Kenyon, 2 vols., New York, Macmillan, 1897.

Orr, Mrs. Sutherland, *Life and Letters of Robert Browning,* revised by Frederic G. Kenyon, Boston, Houghton Mifflin, 1906. (Orr)

Griffin, W. Hall, and Minchin, Harry Christopher, *The Life of Robert Browning,* London, Methuen, 1938. (Griffin & Minchin)

Other Sources Consulted

Browning, Fannie Barrett (Mrs. R. W. B. Browning), *Some Memories of Robert Browning,* Boston, Marshall Jones, 1928.

DeVane, William Clyde, *A Browning Handbook,* New York, Appleton-Century-Crofts, 1955. (DeVane, *Handbook*)

——, *Browning's Parleyings, The Autobiography of a Mind,* New Haven, Yale University Press, 1927.

Gosse, Edmund, *Robert Browning, Personalia,* Boston and New York, Houghton Mifflin, 1890.

Lounsbury, Thomas Raynesford, *The Early Literary Career of Robert Browning,* New York, Scribner's, 1911.

Macready, W. C., *The Diaries of William Charles Macready, 1833–51,* Ed. William Toynbee, 2 vols., London, Chapman and Hall, 1912. (Macready, *Diaries*)

Taplin, Gardner B., *The Life of Elizabeth Barrett Browning,* New Haven, Yale University Press, 1957. (Taplin)

NOTE: The poems used throughout this volume are from *The Complete Poetical Works of Robert Browning,* Cambridge Ed., edited by Horace E. Scudder, Boston, Houghton Mifflin, 1895.

INDEX

ROSEMARY SPRAGUE was born in New York City, but moved to Cleveland, Ohio, when she was about a year old. She admits that she was not overly fond of school. Her parents were aware of this, although they never let her know that they knew until she was in college. She learned to read before she entered the first grade, a discovery which surprised her father and mother as greatly as it annoyed the teacher!

With Cornelia Otis Skinner, she feels she shares the honor of being the most innocent freshman ever to enter Bryn Mawr College. There, she majored in English, took all the languages and history she could and was an active member of the Dramatic Society, choir and glee club.

Following her graduation from Bryn Mawr, she spent a year in New York studying acting with the late Frances Robinson-Duff. Then she entered graduate school at Western Reserve University, where she took her M.A., and was a Fellow-in-English during her last two years' work on her Ph.D. Since receiving her doctorate, she studied at the Shakespeare Institute at Stratford-on-Avon, England, and the University of London. She has been a delegate to the Conference on English Literature at Oxford University in England and to the Conférence Sur des Auteurs Francais at Brussels. She was also a member of the first School of Letters (New Criticism) at Kenyon College.

In 1962 she attended the Shakespeare Seminar at Stratford, Ontario, and delivered a lecture there on "The Men Who Were Not Shakespeare." She has also lectured extensively on children's literature; on Robert Browning; and on Queen Elizabeth I at the Thomas More Institute of the University of Montreal.

She has taught at Western Reserve University; Fenn College, Cleveland, Ohio; The Cleveland Institute of Art; and was director of dramatics at Notre Dame College, South Euclid, Ohio, where she staged the North American premiere of Paul Claudel's *The Satin Slipper.* She is now professor of English at Longwood College, Farmville, Virginia, the oldest women's college in the United States, where she teaches her two specialities, the Victorians and Chaucer. In her spare time, she plays the piano, experiments with gourmet cooking, continues to read incessantly, and goes to the theatre.

Miss Sprague has carved a distinguished career for herself as the author of many historical novels for young adults. *Northward to Albion* was the first and was followed by *A Kingdom to Win,* and *Heroes of the White Shield. Heir of Kiloran* grew out of her love of the theatre and the *commedia del' arte,* in addition to her fascination with the outcome of the intrigues surrounding Mary Stuart. It was named one of the 100 Best Books of 1956 by the *New York Times Book Review.* This was followed by such books as *Conquerors of Time, Dance for a Diamond Star*—concerning Maria de Camargo, the eighteenth-century ballerina—and *The Jade Pagoda,* set in Salem, Massachusetts, in the days of the China trade.

In addition to writing her life of Browning, Rosemary Sprague has recently edited *Poems of Robert Browning.*